What Should I Do if Reverend Billy Is in My Store?

Bill Talen

THE NEW PRESS

NEW YORK
LONDON

Published in the United States by The New Press, New York, 2003
Distributed by W. W. Norton & Company, Inc., New York

LIBRARY OF CONGRESS CATALOGING-IN-PUBLICATION DATA

Billy, Reverend.
    What should I do if Reverend Billy is in my store? / Bill Talen.
      p. cm.
    ISBN 1-56584-824-1 (hc)
    1. Consumption (Economics)—Moral and ethical aspects—United States.
    2. Consumer behavior—Moral and ethical aspects—United States. I. Title.

    HC110.C6B54 2003
    178—dc21

                                                        2003054100

The New Press was established in 1990 as a not-for-profit alternative to the large,
commercial publishing houses currently dominating the book publishing industry.
The New Press operates in the public interest rather than for private gain, and is
committed to publishing, in innovative ways, works of educational, cultural, and
community value that are often deemed insufficiently profitable.

The New Press
38 Greene Street, 4th floor
New York, NY 10013
www.thenewpress.com

In the United Kingdom:
6 Salem Road
London W2 4BU

Composition by Westchester Book Composition

Printed in the United States of America

10 9 8 7 6 5 4 3 2 1

꙼

I ask for one more blessing from my sister Julie Talen and my mother June Talen and her mother Sophie Sieswerda and from my wife Savitri Durkee and our mother Asha Greer and her mother Alice Henry

CONTENTS

il 24, 2000

verend" Billy preaches anti-corporate sentiment in NYC Starbucks locations

Village Voice recently published an article (April 19 – 25, 2000) titled "Rage Against The Caffeine" which ılighted Revered Billy's efforts to wage a campaign against large corporations...particularly Starbucks. ording to the article, Reverend Billy announced a summer campaign in which he'll preach in all Manhattan bucks. Over the past five months, "Reverend" Billy and some of his devotees have entered a few New York / Starbucks locations.

erend Billy sits quietly at a table with devotees and then begins to chat up the customers. He works the crowd า an affirming theme but gradually turns on Starbucks. Towards the end, he's shouting. Then the Reverend's otees hand around anti-Starbucks leaflets. After that, he heads out the door. According to a store manager, he / stand on your tables.

at should I do if Reverend Billy is in my store?
Treat him as any other customer and do not respond to him or his devotees' antics.
Ask him politely to leave the store.
Call the police, if he does not leave.
Page your district manager and marketin███████████████.

estion & Answer
ıo is Reverend Billy?
creation of actor Bill Talen, Reverend Billy began preaching the anti-consumerist gospel in the Times Square ney store three years ago. He wears a white dinner jacket over a black T-shirt and a priest's collar.

at does he say about Starbucks?
verend Billy says that our store's "earth-tone touchy-feeliness masks corporate ruthlessness." The leaflets t he hands out say that Starbucks is screwing the planet, the farmers, the Baristas and New York's ghborhoods.

at should I do if the media comes to my store?
not answer any questions. Nothing is off the record.
er all media inquiries t██████████████.

w do I respond to my customers if they ask how I feel about Reverend Billy's comments?
rbucks has achieved success one cup at a time, one store at a time. We started as a small business in Seattle's e Place market more than 28 years ago. Since then, each one of our stores has become a unique part of its ghborhood. Our stores are about people. The customers and partners (employees) at each location give the 'e its own personality and atmosphere.

ou have any questions, please contact██████████NYC marketing specialist at ███████████.

Reproduction of an internal memorandum circulated by Starbucks Seattle head office to all NYC branches, handed to me after a show by an ex-Starbucks employee.

ACKNOWLEDGMENTS

I started this writing at the Blue Mountain Center, the artist's safehouse in the Adirondacks, and I'm grateful to Harriet Barlow and to her extended family there.

I wish to thank the novelist Charles Gaines, who in regards to this book's chapters, reminded me to tell a story. Jonathan Kalb and Brendan Costello generously helped with these writings as they were pulled from the stage (or sidewalk) toward the page. The radio sermons were the idea of the Creative Producer at WNYC, Marty Goldensohn, and getting a sermon on a single page was a hell of a thing.

The cracked vespers, lifted from the stage shows, reflect the editing of the theater directors who shaped that series of rituals and improvisations over the years: David Ford, Andrew O'Hehir, Vanessa Klimek, Tony Torn, and of course, Savitri Durkee.

I acknowledge the activists who have marched and rallied and been arrested with me, among them Reclaim the Streets, Billionaires for Bush or Gore, the bicyclists of Time's Up, More Gardens! and The Coalition to Save Poe House. The folks at St. Clement's, Judson Church, Charas El Bohio Community Center, Walkerstage and St. Mark's in the Bowery generously lent rehearsal space and base-camps for actions. And thanks especially to Leslie Kauffman, who introduced me to so many of New York City's activists who go forth with their emphatic theater in the streets (and stores).

INTRODUCTION: FUN WITH THE UNKNOWN

In our strange worship at the Church of Stop Shopping we recently took a shiny Sunbeam toaster and put it in the center of the altar.

A young man named Jonah walked up the aisle of the church for his exorcism. As he walked toward the Sunbeam his obvious admiration for it, competing with his faith in the potential of his own buylessness, was very clear. The congregation prayed that he would somehow not grab that sleek chrome bread heater (it resembled a Mercedes coupe and had computerized controls, including a woman's voice that purred "Your toast is done"). I placed my hand on the forehead of this shaking soul as he pleaded with us, "Oh, I don't need your help, I'm just browsing!" How could we possibly blame him for the bald lie? We had positioned the Sunbeam beautifully on a red velvet cloth.

As Jonah reached for the product we prayed hard. The choir hummed and the deacons moved forward to lay hands on the craven consumer as the devil pulled the young man's begging fingers toward the toaster. Jonah was pretty far gone. "Oh . . . toast and butter . . . toast and butter . . . it's more than a smell . . . Oh, my God! Black currant jam on the butter, oh, oh!" The cry was hideous.

But wait! Jonah's hand hesitated, and then pulling out of that force field, it flew back and wavered there in the air. Jonah stared, in shock, at his released fingers. Then he ran around the church as if proving to a Pentecostal TV audience that now he could walk. Held aloft by the preacher, his hand was shaking with new freedom, unburdened. The Stop Shopping Gospel Choir was swaying with the power of a receiptless God-Goddess that surpasseth all valuation. The object looked cheated, cuckolded. Finally the Sunbeam deluxe toaster was just fucking junk.

Not-buying is a brave thing to do. At first it may induce vertigo, identity weirdness, and a desire for an unwanted pregnancy, but most often a new believer will have an abnormal kitsch-acquisition fit. The first response to the break in buying may be a huge sucking sound in your hands—you want to buy something, *anything*. You are headed for a relapse, a spree. My pastoral advice is to steer clear of Ralph Lauren, Kenneth Cole, or any other fashion designer who is trying to anticipate the not-buying revolution by copping a look of weatheredness, offhandedness, or lack of manufacture. Their sales departments think all day about your escape, admiring it and blocking it. They study you via surveillance feeds as they sit in their easy chairs, thoughtfully rubbing their chins.

When you lift your hand from the product and back away from it, a bright, unclaimed space opens up. Consumers think it is a vacuum. It is really only the *unknown*—full of suppressed ocean life, glitterati from Bosch, DNA twists, and childhood quotes that if remembered would burn down the Disney Store.

Many Americans consider this withdrawing gesture a dark thing. Officially, it is absurd, an antigesture, like an American who didn't go west, who didn't go into space, who had sex without a car.

In the Church of Stop Shopping we believe that buying is not nearly as interesting as not-buying. When you back away from the purchase, the product may look up at you with wanton eyes, but it will slump quickly back onto the shelf and sit there trying to get a life. The product needs you worse than you need it—remember that.

Now, if you try this—if you lift your hand from the product, pull that hand back into the aisle, back away from the product, and carefully move toward the door—you may feel turbulence deep in your muscles' memory. You may feel the old grab, the lift, the swipe of plastic, and finally the bagging for the road. The ex-consumer can easily lose his or her footing, buffeted by all those ghost gestures.

Like crack cocaine or membership in the National Rifle Association, shopping is an annihilating addiction that must be slowed down to be stopped. Or flooded with new and different light. But people, please—*do something*! Think of something quick. The research phase is over. How many times do we have to hear that seven percent of the world's population is taking a third of the world's resources? How many neighborhoods need to be malled? When will our foreign policy be violent enough to turn our heads? Recently a local Starbucks rang with shouts of "We are from the Church of the Necessary Interruption!" We will try many strategies. Enacting a purchase in a formal church ritual on Sunday or acting out a comic version of being born again might help those parishioners when they are cornered in Temptation Mall. Sweatshops are truly shocking, and I've seen the sheer force of the information stop a shopper. We make dramas, we sing and shout, and we chain ourselves to Mickey Mouse. We are desperate to access the bright and unclaimed space that the corporations must desperately hide.

In another time, long, long ago, maybe you could have gone ahead and had a life without shopping. But now life without shopping is something that takes years of practice, since shopping is so virulent and ubiquitous that mothers are bathing their wombs with the sounds of Mozart so that their fetuses will score higher on their SATs. Now everything from the most intimate disease to daydreaming is a pretext for the avant-fascism of convenience, comfort, and closure.

We might call that unclaimed space "ordinary life." And how do we design that back in? How much of real life hasn't made it into our fully mediated consumption? Can we ever go home again? We have made thousands of purchases—thousands of times the doors have closed behind us as we walked farther into that big, big sale.

The bumper sticker says Birth, Shopping, Death. Well, birth and death are a part of ordinary life. And ordinary life is itself amazing; the intriguing mystery that precedes birth and follows death does not stop when we are alive. Perhaps the great con began when the churches made us pay for our own arrival and departure. Life itself has as much unknown in it as death; it is just as inexplicable. That's the thrill of the ride. We say, Put the ODD Back in GOD!

We shop because we fear life. We shop because we want to banish from life something we identify with death, the unknown. It waits for us in that bright, unclaimed space. Of course, we are trained to think of what we can't know as a bad thing. Actually, it is the source of the brightness; it is why this space has no owner.

The unknown will circle around and insert itself throughout this book. While I'm claiming that the rejection of living-by-products opens up a sensual and peopled life, yet it does have in it an acceptance of the unknown, which is always waiting with the glorious indifference of the fires that float above us in the night sky. Is it a contradiction that accepting this unknown is what makes it possible for us to live together? Well, there is nothing more thoroughly mysterious than love, thank God. Those who organize defenses against the Unknown (such as religious fundamentalists and consumer fundamentalists) foment numbness, hatred, and war. Unfortunately, they have perfected their imitation of ordinary living, and that comes to us as the comforting ghost gesture of shopping.

Ordinary life will feel counterintuitive, to put it mildly. But what will happen to the American consumer when the consuming stops is about as fascinating a question as we can ask.

Imagine this ecstatic release from consumerism taking place inside a Starbucks.

ONE:

THE PILEATED WOODPECKER SCREAMS

I roll out of bed, and for a minute or two I have no idea what day it is. Just a Sunday, is what I'm thinking. Everybody slows down on Sunday; lots of folks don't even leave the house. Maybe I'll just stay in bed and read whatever book I can reach.

I'm wandering around, rubbing my face, making my way gravely to the espresso roast. My black cat, Ronita, looks at me with an absence of respect or even of recognition. Then it hits me—today is the day of an action. My eyebrows leap, my face gapes, my hands grope in the air for a cardboard sword or someone's throat or the window latch.

The day of an action. I go to the window and look down five stories, and there it is—very much a Sunday at 7 a.m. There is no one down there. The bleary pavement gives off no signals. On the cornice of the dark building opposite me are four stone faces, and they all have the same astonished expression. But the thing that surprised these gargoyles must have happened a century ago, because there's nothing going on now. Still, there is a menacing quality in this gray erasure of a dawn; there's an implied unknown, as if something may arrive at any minute with its own laws.

This empty Sunday is like photographs of New York architecture that don't have any people in them. You stare at the image and expect a crowd to rush in, everybody in a hurry. Everything has happened down in this street: My cat and I have seen lovemaking and even a murder from this window. But the city is always incomplete. As the coffee hits, I want to know—what's missing that I have to do? The action. I'm standing here with heroic fear from head to toe.

What am I afraid of? Well, how would you describe the multinational corporations? They are powerful, like parents, but they are like parents we haven't quite met. They have the legal status of persons, and in their advertising they pretend that they are chummy relatives or lovers, but the power imbalance is so extreme that they can deny their parenthood anytime they want to. Their corruption of the legal and political systems and their regimentation of culture are near complete now, and ever more unnoticed. We are at the point in consumer culture that I remember from the civil rights struggle—the point where assimilation is just over, we're disappearing, let's get out of here! Let's . . . let's . . . be rude! And so—how do we push away? And so how to push away? How to even see any withdrawal of the corporate life at all? Our affinity group, our "church," will try to slide between a group of people and the cash register of Starbucks, the fastest-growing brand name in the world. We'll try to pull them apart.

I'm looking at my preacher's costume, the $5 priest's collar hanging by the choir robes. We'll pry potential sippers from a set of gestures, from the completion of a contract. We'll insert the word of the concocted God of Stop Shopping into the Starbucks at Astor Place, the biggest $bucks in Manhattan. I will be an interruption today. A candidate for the Tombs, Manhattan's medieval cellar of detention. I'll be doing the wrong thing as loudly as possible with the Stop Shopping Gospel Choir and a French television crew.

I have done this before, political acting on the sloppy stage of someone else's property. I know it is not easy to do well. The trespassed space is so charged that once you go in it's hard to remember what you wanted to say, it's hard to say it if you remember it, and it's hard to hear it if you say it. But somehow tragicomic invasions of the underwater cave of the mermaid with no nipples are something that we are driven to do again and again. And so this Sunday morning, as I have these memories of previous break-ins of the retail calm of chain stores, I say hello to my history of extreme embarrassment like it's an old buddy who vomits in my elevator.

The Astor Place Starbucks has become our stage. How could it not? This pale imitation of an avant-garde café blended with a touch of the sanitized mall? We go into these privatized commons, with wave upon wave of intense, precision fools. Actions. The Guerrilla Girls, Andy Kaufman—all the people who stop us to start us. Jesus and Mary. Time's Up. Reclaim the Streets. The Sex Pistols. Mayakovsky. Muhammad Ali. The ACT UP guy who started yelling in the White House about the man he loved. The Boston Tea Party. Let's say—Abbie Hoffman on the balcony of the New York Stock Exchange, throwing money down on the frothing, teeth-gnashing traders. When have we needed these citizens of change more than now, in the most drab and violent era since Joe McCarthy?

Already it's too late for Sunday, that romantic day of rest. That's destroyed, never to return. My invocation of centuries of inappropriate behavior, in a fateful combination with my 100 percent fair trade espresso roast Peace Coffee, makes me want to play loud music—Chicago blues like Buddy Guy, Otis Rush, Magic Sam. The empty city wants a good shout.

I like to shout this: "First they ignore you, then they laugh at you, then they fight you, then they lose." It's Gandhi. He probably whispered it. But it works with a hip-hop rhythm.

> "First they ignore you, then they laugh at you,
>   then they fight you, then they lose . . .
> "First they ignore you, then they laugh at you,
>   then they fight you, then they lose . . . "

Starbucks is somewhere between ignoring and fighting, having skipped the laughing—it is nothing if not humorless. In fact, the first thing you can say about chain stores and malls, all those overcommodified "planned communities," is that no one there can really *play*.

Starbucks is worse than most because it is entirely unaware of the contrast between its corporate drabness and the glamorous history of café life that it employs as an enticement to customers. No, Starbucks is not funny. But in the way that Puritans stalk the sexually active, it is haunted by funny. When the Starbucks scouts come into a neighborhood you can picture them walking around with their ears cocked—they are listening for the sound of laughter. Where is the heated story-making taking place, where are the jokes being told? Then they go to the landlord of the diner or the shop from which the sounds of life are emanating. If they can't break the lease, they'll lay siege to a happening spot with an empty Starbucks next door. They can easily absorb the losses. (We dub them "attack cafés." Even they call it cannibalizing the neighborhood, as Naomi Klein reports in *No Logo*.) All they want to do is pick off 5 percent of the target diner's clientele, the less dedicated ones, like tourists. These attacks often succeed because stand-alone indy businesses generally have a narrow margin between income and costs.

Starbucks is the classically predatory multinational corporation. At Astor Place, where we're headed today, three branches are located at the same intersection.

I'm feeling the whole day now. I've been able to order my emotions somewhat. When I start the Gandhi hip-hop chant I always end up in the rhythms of the sidewalk preachers. Both the rapper and the preacher are helpful for the focus of our strategic embarrassment in today's political action. They are hard-core singer/talkers who reclaim public space. If they are embarrassed for a moment, it's only a door they walk through. I'll try to remember to use the Gandhi mantra as a warm-up for the choir. They'll be coming up to the apartment soon.

I go to the window and see Sunday morning people slowly entering the sunlight. They're walking down on the street and I experience the hair-raising fear that I had when I got out of bed. These sleepy couples, walking off their alcoholic haze or their Sunday morning news show. Why do they trouble me? Why are my eyebrows leaping again, my eyes boggling? Well, they might be the same people we will interrupt later today, in Starbucks. They will somehow collaborate in this action with us. Their understanding of the script may be to act as witnesses to the police, but they will be on our stage. When I am reincarnated as a lefty Jimmy Swaggart, holy-rolling some virulent politics about shopping, wrapping it in a Pentecostal joke, these sleepy people will be interrupted. Interrupt: into the rupture. Not the Rapture, the Rupture.

Here comes the choir. The deacons and singers are arriving from the Village and Williamsburg and Newark, pushing the buzzer in the lobby. Waiting in our tin can of an elevator and listening to those chains uncoiling. I can hear the Amens growing in the hallway, Brother Derrick and Sister Julie and Brother James are post-legato and going native. *Will someone give me an outlashing of Oddness! Oh honey have you got some Sanctified Oddness for me?* The casual hallelujahs are coming through the door, the cat goes into hiding, and the Stop Shopping Gospel Choir is supporting the column of air with the diaphragm and hitting the downbeat with the hips and Brother Benny Key the music director is scolding them into a frenzy. "We're gonna put that cappuccino down! Stop Shopping! Stop Bombing!"

A political statement is ringing in the air, in the form of simple joy. Things make so much sense after the singing starts. Heads are tilted up and arms are open—you can't really argue with this. I believe that this will deprogram a consumer in the middle of a pseudo hip sip.

This is the right sort of interruption, because it's not an interruption at all—it's removing something that was shadowing the joy that is there in all of us. The corporation people must wonder when we'll catch on. They are the bigger talker, the more apparently convinced, with their voices that radiate from the horizon right into our doubled-over conscience. But they must know—our own joy could take us away from their products at any moment. Okay, I'm ready. This is that moment. My quiet fear is burned off by the heat of this holy Odd singing. My terror at dawn just seems funny.

Now we descend into the street. Amen.

We're walking uptown, a preacher, a sunshiny choir, and a few deacons, about twenty-five of us in all. We're walking up our main street, which is Lafayette, up a canyon of horny-looking supermodels. Some of them are only six feet tall and in the flesh, some of them are ten stories and draped down the sides of buildings. They are imploring us to buy clothing, accessories, things that appear on our bodies in miniature down here far below. Construction is everywhere, bricks in piles, and skeletons of tenements becoming stylish town houses. And at the end of all this "development" awaits a vast coffee shop symbolizing prosperity (to some) at a famous intersection where two avenues and three streets come together.

The Astor Place Starbucks. In the pantheon of neighborhoods that they've ruined, this must be a trophy. Where to start? On the east edge of Astor is Cooper Union, where Abe Lincoln spoke in 1860. His speech to 1,500 tough New Yorkers was mesmerizing; he was carried out by the throng and into his presidency. Yes, and moving forward 120 years, ACT UP met in Cooper Union throughout the AIDS crisis. Of all the history in Cooper Union's Great Hall, the brazen shouters of ACT UP are especially saints in our church. No activism now is possible without ACT UP. Silence equals death.

And then down Lafayette a short way is the home of the Public Theater of Joe Papp and his remarkable full cycle of the Bard's plays, the birthplace of *A Chorus Line* and *For*

Colored Girls Who Have Considered Suicide When the Rainbow Is Enuf. And just uptown and more than a century ago—where the Kmart now stands—the Astor Opera House imposed its cultural will by casting a British actor in the role of Hamlet, and twenty-three Bowery Boys were shot as they rioted over the snubbing of the American who wanted the part. Imagine that.

The traffic island with the black cube sculpture balanced on its tip attracts skateboarders in swarms like flies, and the tourists of the world stand here looking out as their guides shout the bold type of history, Lincoln, Papp, the Bowery Boys. But there isn't much to look at anymore. The buildings whose angels and gnarled forest men and all those stone faces that have watched us blunder through time below them—they are covered with logos now.

This commons has such energy in its walls that it has attracted the global slap of the advertisers' plastic, unending . . . repetitive . . . the visual drum machine of fluorescent logos. Stand on the traffic island and turn slowly. If you start facing due north and move counterclockwise, the first thing you'll see is Old Navy's huge sign, next is the Kmart (with the angry Bowery Boy ghosts milling around), the big Starbucks where we are headed, then the Kinko's, the Gap, Barnes and Noble, with a Starbucks on the second floor of course, and then if you continue spinning around you'll see three enormous puppies with overturned spaghetti on their heads, a sign for the new Disney remake, then the McDonald's, and finally the third Starbucks. Now local wags call Astor Place the "Bermuda Triangle of retail." You can disappear in here and *they won't even find your bones.*

We walk into Astor Place with the choir choreographer Brother James Benn going over moves with a new singer, and the conductor Mother Dee Spencer eyeing the two-level supercafé with its Sunday crowd. The place is imposing, but its pretension is undermined by the cliché of signature earth tones. The French TV crew are crouching behind their gunlike cameras. We hide in a side street, waiting for the signal from our "action manager," who sits behind the plate glass with the Buckheads.

First, we pray. I've found that whatever the occasion, whenever I'm in trouble, it helps to honor the people who aren't there. The people who support us but are not with us, whether they are long gone or still living—we ask for their guidance. I don't know why this always feels right. It's almost enough to make an ironist believe. I think that we all want to bring back the people who are gone, or those we feel are not gone but should be re-revealed.

The choir is ready to pray and go. They're nervous too. All right. So we gather like a football team, with our hands clasped one over the other, in a tall stack. "*Oh children let us pray to the God that is not a product. We ask that our message go straight into the sky, past the logo-barnacled walls, up past Cindy Crawford's lip mole. And we ask to be protected and blessed by those whose stories are buried beneath this overlay of logos. The long-ago dead left us these sculpted lionesses and snakes and angels—and they watch over us and we say thank you for this. And . . . we ask for the blessing of the family that ran the Astor Riviera Diner—evicted from this corner by the speculator lawyers of Starbucks. And . . . we ask for the power from the old impatient waiters in their bad tuxes. Amen.*"

The action manager Vera Beren is inside now and she gives us our two-if-by-land signal. The choir is filing in, William Henry in the lead with his battery-powered Korg organ. I'm watching from the sidewalk out front as William places the instrument on a table, sits, takes the black vinyl case off the black and white keys, turns up the volume, and, after checking first with Dee, starts hitting the gospel chords with his long fingers. The choir faces Mother Dee. She looks like Moms Mabley on amphetamines. Her baton is now circling in the air with the beat. I can barely hear it from where I'm standing out front, but I can tell it's *got the spirit*. This is the beginning of the performance, where those who don't know our work must think we're crazy Christians on a proselytizing weekend in New York, the evil city. They imagine our bus around the corner and wait for our End Times booklets.

The Stop Shopping Gospel Choir is singing big now, moving in syncopation with their arms up like wings, and the rousing chorus of "Put your latte down!" is causing a radiating wave of double takes through this cafeteria of derivative hipness. The deacons are circulating with their flyers and invitations to go elsewhere for coffee. Vera nods at me. It is time to preach. But I'm not ready.

I'm out there in front, gleaming in the late-night cable preacher getup with the priest's collar, my hair megaheld toward the sky. And I'm frozen. I'm standing there like a Reverend Billy action figure that's out of batteries. I can see Vera standing inside. Café customers in the windows see Reverend Billy and stare in silent expectation. I duck behind the news kiosk to gather myself.

I've reverted to the state of shock I was in when I woke up this morning. I've stopped at the border of private property, frightened by the requirement that I breach it. Going inside was my idea; I talked everybody into it. And now my collaborators are in there, putting themselves at risk, and I'm stuck outside, terrified. I need power. I *need* power. So I'm praying again. The guy selling his wares in the little hut of mags and papers nearby on the sidewalk thinks I'm a priest. He leaves me alone. I just need power. I don't usually hesitate like this.

I'm trying to work out the source of the fear. Fear of what? The ordinary conversation in the café, the people with their crossed legs ready to be annoyed, the carefully Starbucks-calibrated amber light, the apparent complacent happiness in there, the interruption I am committed to—I'm spooked. I feel how *inappropriate* this all is. I don't know what to do. I have to go to my Odd God prayer again, always at the ready for emergencies. O Mystery Thing—I'm addressing the part of the sky not covered over with swooshes, arches, crosses, swastikas, sepulchres, dollar signs, or George Bush's pet pillow . . . I pray for a Godsighting. Something vivid, one of my chosen stories, or an image, a sign, a glance. James Brown says, "Swing on the vine, check out your mind." Let me swing. Amen.

I can hear the choir are into their second song. But I'm in trouble. It's not coming. Maybe it's robot time. Just phone it in, as the actors say. I'm leaning on the news hut with my eyes closed. Abe Lincoln and Joe Papp and all you sculpted beings peering down—lend me your gravitas. Amen.

Vera comes out, and my sermon coach Tony Torn is now here too. They're both asking me what's the matter? I tell them I need a little time. The choir is ripping into its third song:

"Let me lift my hand! Let me turn my head! O Lord, I got Nike swooshes in my underwear! Oh, help me!" Would it be so bad if it was just an anti-consumerist gospel concert this time, without a preacher? It sounds great in there. "O Lord, take this cup of sweatshop coffee from me." Vera and Tony give me the same withering look.

I watch the choir with their liquidy golden robes inside the windows of the coffee shop. They are so wrong in there. It looks like an aquarium or something. I don't notice I've drifted back into the street. The horns of the taxis disharmonize like a brass section falling off a cliff. Tony and Vera pull me back into the news hut.

What was that? Oh. That's it. All right—there it is. I stand still and close my eyes. An old memory. Wait. Yes, the God-sighting I asked for. I can barely make it out. This is coming from decades ago, from deep in the forest. A great shadow crossing in front of me. It's a bird, a great bird—the size of a raven or a loon. It's perched up on the branch of an old dead tree full of holes. How my mind is spinning. I must have been, what, ten years old? This creature. It's got a white and black slashed zebra face with a fiery red crest. It's like a great radical drag queen straight from the dark part of the forest. Feathers hanging down like Count Dracula's cloak. It is power and it is ODD.

This is the famous Pileated Woodpecker. I remember that as a child I wanted to see one for years. But it never came to town; it doesn't like "development." And then I remember it made a scream with its face opening like a terrible pair of scissors. You see I don't have to talk myself into this action. I'm going in there and I'm not coming from dialectical theo-retical politics. I've got a crazy animal from the forest up my id, in my odd, the totemic personality that's got it all over the green mermaid. Ooh, Vera? Tony? I'm ready to testify! *I've got my portable Pileated Count Dracula Black-bellied Woodpecker God!* Can I preach today? Oh, yeah.

I thank the newspaper vendor and follow Tony and Vera back in and I am silently raising my arms as I walk by the impassive mermaid and through the door. See, that wasn't so bad—I'm going to fly. The choir is stealing glances at the preacher but I'm going to be fine. "Don't worry, I can fly." Walking through the couples, through the little bands of friends, walking up to the counter where the cappuccino machine hisses, turning around and facing a roomful of arrested leisure time. I have never been so ready to INTERRUPT. I just feel loud sounds rolling up through me and I take off flapping and soaring over the tables.

I'm soaring over the steaming little ponds of beverage on the tables. And I'm soaring over the coffee plantations in Guatemala, looking down and seeing the families who tend the living coffee. I'm sensing their entrapment in these products. And I'm saying to them and myself that I'll do my best. First I go to the choir to get Julie and Maria and Mr. Glover and Ruby and David and Linnette and James and Toya and Dominic and Taiyi and June and Sonja and Jerry and Michelle's blessings, and, yes, the choir is laughing and this feels fine.

It feels real fine to be walking on what Starbucks says is its "private property." I'm the KING OF THE TREESTABBERS and I'm about to share the message with these consumer sinners. We have a momentary staredown, as they peer up from their multinational corporate foam.

"I COME BEARING GLAD TIDINGS: YOU ARE NOT REALLY BUCKHEADS! YOU'RE JUST IN HELL, THAT'S ALL—Hell defined as sitting here fibrillating on minor drugs surrounded by fake avant-garde wallpaper. Is there anyone here, children, is there anyone here who is not SICK TO DEATH OF GOOD GRAPHICS? Look at these walls, these impossibly hip earth tones. Is it Jean-Michel Basquiat? Well, not . . . NOT QUITE. But he used to live in this neighborhood! And this decor, doesn't it look very Robert Rauschenberg? This looks like his photomontage work. Oh, but no, it's actually ALMOST RAUSCH-ENBERG BUT NOT QUITE! But his studio was right here on Bond Street. No this is LIKE the neighborhood, it is IN the neighborhood, but it IS NOT the neighborhood. It's Starbucks, and where is that? Where is Starbucks? IT'S NO PLACE.

"In fact, we are tourists in our own lives, there's a disconnect. Our words have a barely discernible echo. We have the same relation to living real lives that these art-school Starbucks graphics have to the real artists who lived on this street. WE'RE IN THE FAKE CAFÉ, AND WE CAN'T KNOW THE REAL COST OF THAT LATTE!"

Now the manager's lips are spraying spit in my ear as he mouths, *"Police!"* The congregation before me is dividing into several camps: There are the unrepentant sinners who frown and concentrate hard on their Frappuccinos, there are the loving-this people who clap along with the choir, the ubiquitous cellphoners who turn away to face the wall. Then there are those for whom we are New York characters to be captured on their tourist cameras, and a more sinister group who are also recording us on film—the corporate executives who will view the surveillance tapes at Starbucks' Seattle HQ.

The manager has turned up the volume of the Muzak machine. But that's naive, I'm loud. The choir is irresistible. We are ripping open this thick, gauzy mood. Who and what is this preacher? Carry Nation with her ax? John the Baptist standing in the middle of the river screaming in his G-string? *"Now, let's talk. Children, I live here. Can I talk to you without a corporation's mediation for just a moment? Let's make a decision. Do we want to cooperate with them?"*

I decide to keep moving, following the deacons who are handing out the flyers. I channel the flyer, I sing the flyer electric: *"Starbucks has a long history of buying coffee from plantations where they employ families at slave wages, where the monoculture-and-pesticides approach to raising coffee has replaced shade-growth biodiverse farming . . . then they add unhealthy genetically altered milk . . . Howard Schultz . . . nearing his first billion . . . coffee workers . . . impoverished . . . has used prison labor to package Starbucks products . . . surveilling labor reps at the roasting plants . . ."*

There is a part of my mind that is watching the coffee drinkers at their little circular tables, mostly those aforementioned Sunday couples, although there are also one or two families with children and strollers, waiting for the wild church to blow over. I don't preach over them. I try to look into everyone's eyes and sometimes it becomes all one eye. A vortex of witnessing and weighing the meaning that they are building in themselves—my argument that we are sitting in a financial bubble that has hurt people who are not here. Once again, the people who are not here.

The choir is filing out past the mermaid, back out to the street, singing and hip-rocking like a conga line, the Parisian camera people dancing with them. Vera is staring down the manager, and Tony is standing there like a football coach on the sidelines. And then suddenly several cops are walking toward me. I look up and I'm eye to eye with the mermaid. This is the defining moment of the entire day, the moment that came to me when I woke up in a state of shock. But the Pileated Woodpecker is still strong in me, a strange huge bird with a face that screams I AM VERY ODD AND I SURVIVE EVERYTHING AND AS I GET STRANGER I GET STRONGER. With the manager pawing my back, I have tripped into an old memory that has a high-powered totemic kick.

"Let us pray." I'm on my knees. The cops are hesitating. I ask the one who's closest to me, *"Do you buy Starbucks coffee?"* He says, *"Too expensive."* I say, *"Well, Starbucks blew away a family that ran a diner here for fifteen years, and you know there's no lease protection for anybody in this town. Yeah, Starbucks was too expensive for them, too. And you guys have a strong union, but you know Starbucks doesn't have a union. Look, give me a second, I'll leave. But officer, let me tell you I'm full of a very hairy childhood memory right now—some part of me honestly believes that I am a giant woodpecker. Maybe you think I'm a preacher with a church. But I gotta Odd God! I got Mahatma Gandhi and Johnny Rotten and James Brown coursing through my veins. You don't even want me in the Tombs."*

And the police pause for a moment, discussing the situation among themselves. Time is slowing down like it does when your car is in a skid and it is clear that you are in an accident but it hasn't happened yet. I do a 360 turn in the Astor Place Starbucks and take in the hundreds of eyes, the open faces that were in conversations of wit or despair or boredom now turned toward this Fool who wants them to stand up and shatter the skein of a thousand little arrangements. *"Children! While the ex-hippie monsters in Seattle watch in horror, walk, children! Pick up what is left of your true self and walk, walk slowly toward the door, follow me out . . . and then, and then we will run!"*

Yes, my Billy Graham climax. "Come down here in front. We will wait for you." One well-dressed couple gets up to join me, and then some more people who appear to hesitate at first and then become more convinced. These folks are, in fact, part of our troupe. We call them the icebreakers.

"Starbucks children—SAVE YOURSELVES FROM SHOP-PING! O God Almighty, SAVE US FROM CONSUMER HAPPINESS, the vague pleasantness of HIPNESS BY DE-FAULT!"

The cops are herding the flying Fool toward the door. I feel the eyes around the room on my back and turn around. I have a sudden compassion for everyone here, stuck on this Sunday morning in a place that mocks them and makes them pay for it. *"People, I just marvel at how we keep this up. How do we handle the torturous appraisal that this is somehow okay? We all feel why it isn't. We know better. Of course we do."*

I'm nearing the door and shaking hands and I feel tender-ness for these people. The cops allow me to slow down in order to clasp outstretched hands and receive little thank-yous like preachers always do at the end of a service. I make a final turn at the door.

"The Astor Riviera Diner is still here—we remember it, and here it comes! See it? We are standing in it! It is returning! Does anyone here remember the old diner's abusive waiters? Wonderful."

We go back out into Astor Place, and I'm glad to say some

souls are saved that night. People put their lattes down and join us on the traffic island. We sing and sing in our own portable commercial-free zone.

We're trying to find the thing called neighborhood, called *community* . . . we're looking for it on the sidewalks out here, trying to reawaken it in the heart of commodification. Once we return to public space, I can feel the eyes of the logos looking down at us, the actors and models selling their perfumes and cars from the high walls of the city. We have flouted them, and they gaze on, impassively. But behind them are the older, darker eyes of abandoned gods, huntresses, satyrs, angels—the faces left to us by hands that have disappeared into the air. They have witnessed what we have done, together with Abe and Joe and the crowd that bustled through here when Walt Whitman was drinking down at his favorite bar, just there on Lafayette and Bleecker.

I see my godless God flying over the commons, the fabulously Odd Pileated Woodpecker. It occurs to me that my king of the forest probably hasn't lived on this island since notorious slumlord John Jacob Astor resided in that big mansion over the street.

We come back to my apartment and get the robes hung. Toast our action. I'm fading now, ready to sleep. And yes, this was a hell of a Sunday. But Sunday's a day of work for a preacher.

Letter to "the Starbucks employee who must read this," addressed in care of Howard Schultz, founder and chairman of Starbucks, May 23, 2002

Dear Bucksurveillor:

At the turn of the millennium there is a growing sense that a massive fraud has been perpetrated and right now the evidence is . . . boredom.

Why else would your customers jump up and dance with our choir? You've surveilled this. You've interviewed your employees. You see that in the file, don't you? Maybe you yourself tapped your foot as you watched the tape.

I have in my computer the image of your mermaid when she still had her nipples, from the days before you considered them an affront, as it were, to the possibly upset conservatives in Akron and Memphis and Dubai. And so the nipples were quietly airbrushed by executive fiat. And you think, how could this matter? Well, we have found that when a woman from the Church of Stop Shopping stands up in the middle of your coffee shop and shouts, "I am the mermaid and I want my nipples back!" there is instant recognition across the café. Volunteer actresses (and actors) have lifted their voices in Vancouver, and Iowa City, and Providence—they want the human body wholly returned. There is the initial laughter and then an unmistakable wise silence. You have airbrushed our desire in all directions, but if the customers remember their hots, the goddess comes out of the wall. The dead begin to move.

This coffee—it radiates its sensual past, too. What can you do to stop it? The pure products of America go crazy. The object itself testifies. The mermaid flips her hair over her shoulder. From the families in the Americas tending the soil as it creates the complex magic of the original plant, to the family evicted from this corner, your own product carries a long life that reveals its own beautiful hidden flesh.

See you in the store . . .

Reverend Billy

POSTSCRIPT TO A SCREAM

About the Pileated Woodpecker: I was a bird-watcher when I was a kid and I was alone a lot. Now that I'm getting older, these long-dead feathered souls are soaring with me for my political performances. I've been doing these actions more and more, and I now have been revisited by Storks, Anhingas, Loons, Pelicans, Ravens . . . Their presence seems to make the vulnerable ego something I can leave at home.

Lately I've been wondering why. Why these birds? Well, first, maybe I'm imitating them when I preach, because they make tremendous screams, hoots, maniacal laughs. (If you listen to a good Pentecostal preacher on the radio and you turn off the American English in your mind, so he or she is just making sounds, you hear squawking and cooing like some unappeased wet bird in a tree.)

Or maybe the aviary of memories has power for me because the species that I love are disturbingly eccentric. Night herons, fish eagles, snowy owls. They have mutated happily away from the mainstream pigeon in the street.

Let's say, for the sake of argument, that there is a kind of complex image that is very important, not just a shard of color, more than a coincidence: It is a *Chosen Story*. Each of us has an identity because we are a sum total of our Chosen Stories. Say that the irreproducible thing that a few of you recognize as "Bill Talen" is the creation of 713 hair-raising stories. Most of them come from experiences I've had in my life, or dreamy fictions based in events—but really, who knows?—they are the Chosen Stories. I have retained them as physical information.

Some of the 713 are traumatic, some glorious. The most influential ones took place when I was younger.

Sometimes, for some reason—this ever happen to you?—I'll be walking along and I'll have memory after memory that I swear I haven't thought of in 10 or 20 years. They'll come in a binge, like a mad projectionist can't stop showing them: suddenly I'm twelve, I see a cat kill a rabbit and so I take the cat by the tail and whip it up into the sky; I'm eight or nine years old in another memory—I think a man is my father and I catch myself only after I jump into the front seat of his car, I'm staring into his eyes; and here comes another—I'm older in this one—I'm sleeping in a basement listening to jazz on a yellow plastic radio and I'm imagining somehow flying over the clouds on the power of these notes back to the cities that originate them and I want to escape . . .

And on and on—then I'll shudder with this view of the vast landscape of the 713 stories and wonder hard about the process of how, from them, I came to believe in some things, fear others, and build up my homegrown collection of intuitions. My gestures, how deep I breathe. My odd pause, when I stop to look at a thing. From my birth these chosen stories steered me on my march to Billyness. They are my narrative DNA.

When I received the memory of that Pileated Woodpecker, with my younger self jumping with the happy shock of seeing this thing come out of the woods like death in *The Seventh Seal*, the story was pushing back the general amnesia. I was "remembering who I am." Underneath all the political/aesthetic/ethical arguments that make this revolution against Consumerism necessary it always comes back to the simple act of waking up this way. The ad departments would like to supply us with those 713 stories themselves, or at least delete the ones that lead us away from their products.

In our political action that day at Astor Place we were trying to trespass both ways. We were trespassing into ourselves to steal back our forgotten life while at the same time marching forward into those dominant, commercial narratives. If we remember ourselves, we save our city.

THE READER WILL PLEASE RISE

It is now time in our service for the recitation of "Can You Believe This?"

Sing this all on one note, with the high-pitched resolved anguish of Episcopalian sad-sack Christianity. At the dash near the end of the line, take a breath, then sing the last part of the phrase also on that same note.

Ready?

> We believe in the God that people who don't believe in God—believe in.
> We believe in shopping the way that people who never shop—do their shopping.
> We believe that Convenience—is not convenient.
> We believe that supermodels are—state terrorism.
> We believe that to stop crime you don't have to—kill your city.
> We believe that you didn't have to squeeze me but you did, but you did—but you did.
> We believe that if a sweatshop worker finds out that one morning of Michael Eisner's income would feed her family for ten lifetimes, then Eisner is already closer than he realizes to being—forced to share.

Take one big breath and say it fast:

> We believe in the return of the indy bookstore, mom-and-pop apothecaries, small vendors, sex workers, and stoops with open containers that have liquid

content of all kinds and where you might have to
stop and weather the feeling that you are wasting
time and find yourself telling a story or—being
told a howler that you might have to retell with
your own adornments and expurgations.

The reader will be seated.
Children! Can you believe this?

The idea of preaching started in the dark.

TWO:

THE RED CHAIR

I shudder to think when Reverend Billy started. I was so outside of time then, and I was out of place. In those days I was never on time—I was late or I was early. And if you looked hard at my face, you'd say, "I'm trying to place you."

If I was any place at all, it was a red chair in a church. I was sitting in an old red overstuffed chair, yes, and it had an odor. It smelled like generations of people had passed out in this chair, pissed, smoked, used hair spray, and spilled God knows what party chemicals into the sedimentation in the seams of the bloodred vinyl. I was seated there for a long, long time; it was a stock-still campaign of sitting—or, no, flopping—all night in this chair up at the altar of St. Clement's Episcopal Church.

"Sitting" suggests meditation. "Flopping" suggests passing out or squatting without paying rent. I was up at the altar doing all these things. In a church at night, I was waiting for . . . well, what—God? I don't think so. I was in the church because I worked there and lived there. Beyond the altar fetish, my intentions were not too precise. Put it this way—I wasn't sleeping well.

And it wasn't because I couldn't turn the lights off. It was always dark in St. Clement's, whatever time it was, because the shutters stayed closed on the stained-glass windows unless I opened them, and even then the stained glass was caked with soot from the permanent traffic jam on Ninth Avenue in the approach to the Lincoln Tunnel.

St. Clement's is a raffish little house of God on West Forty-sixth, deep in Hell's Kitchen, hard by the theater district. It is both a place of worship and a theater. Think about that: The altar is also a stage. This church averages fewer than a hundred dues-paying members, so renting out the stage is an important moneymaker. The theater companies sign up for their performances a year in advance, without telling the church what comedy or tragedy is moving in.

During the service, the priest, praying in a lifted voice to God Almighty, stands in the middle of the current play's set, which might be the tenement kitchen of *Look Back in Anger*, with a big dirty sink and the sensation that a hairy Method actor in a dirty T-shirt is about to enter belching stage left. The contradictions loom. If you are taking communion in St. Clement's, you could find yourself looking up from your knees in the middle of the set of *No Exit*, Sartre's depiction of hell.

These devilish props give the awesome eternal life of God an unfortunate rental quality. The believers face the priest in the sheening purple clerical robes, with the raised hands and the intoning voice, but all the candles and Eucharists are portable and the holy cross comes down from the rafters on a pulley system, lowered like a flag on a pole every Sunday morning.

I was the house manager at the theater. I had the keys to the place, and I lived with my dog, Jessica, in a little ten-by-ten room up under the church spire. And I couldn't sleep.

I would go down to the dark house of worship. Every night I'd haul out the mysterious red chair. I'd pull it from a closet off the stage wing and sit there, downstage center. I would open the long Gothic doors that enclosed the stained-glass windows—I opened them because the windows were so beautiful at night: the lambs of God, the haloed doves, the angels' curling fabric flowing in the blissful wind of heaven, all softly glowing from the heated hell of the city.

On my way to the red chair I would look at the set of the current production and then turn off the lights. I wouldn't be able to resist the reality of the play. Maybe I'd be sprawled out in a prairie motel room, with one of Sam Shepard's lunatic family dramas resonating in the air around me. I'd sit there each night for six weeks. Then there would be a load-out and a load-in and I'd have to switch channels to some underfinanced facsimile of an Ibsenesque drawing room. Jessica and I would come and go for another six weeks. Then suddenly I'd be sitting all night in a medieval forest, with the spit of hardworking Shakespearean actors all over the floor.

This went on month after month, through the night, waking up and dozing off. Jessica would walk by and try to communicate something, then lie down and fall asleep, and her legs would start twitching as she chased a dream deer across a distant meadow. Sometimes I would wake up and check the doors to make sure no one was jimmying their way in. I'd always check the ten-foot-tall crucifix tied up in the flies. I could hear the rats hesitate inside the old walls as I walked by.

I would return to the comforting Dionysian stench of the great red chair. I couldn't put the stained-glass imagery out of my mind—the crosses and praying hands and lambs of God had an incandescence in the room. My free fall through life left me with a whole new broadcast form.

Was I unhappy? No, I wasn't unhappy. Listen, unhappiness is underrated. Lots of people swear by unhappiness. Millions live their entire lives that way and on their deathbeds they feel vindicated. Sure, I was unhappy—what's it to ya? I was another anonymous new New Yorker, arrived from an immigrant's Oceania with a headful of New York foreshadowings in a mind that was trying too hard.

And what was New York City showing me? I came to Broadway, what I thought was the center of any actor's world, and I was crushed to discover that theater no longer existed there. I had moved across the country with all the expectations that can be assigned to New York City. Okay, here I am—now where's the show? I've put my last $70 down on a great seat at a Broadway opening night. The curtain rises and there, center stage, in hat and tails, tonight's celebrity host: MICKEY FUCKING MOUSE.

I got back to the old red chair with the fumes in the middle of a church in the middle of a play. I'd sit and wait and wait into the predawn, when the sound and the fury of the city would almost go to emptiness. There was always a mysterious light that would shine in through the cracks of the church, like a cop with a flashlight in the window when you fell asleep in the backseat with your high school sweetheart.

The source of the prying light would be the reified teeth of Mickey Mouse, enforced by the good clean violence of Mayor America. Even before Disney got its manifest destiny and tax breaks, Rudy Giuliani was pushing back the ghouls of a Broadway gone dark (in his dark view) with the superweapon of the rat's dental work. With relish he demonized the community, Forty-second Street, four-deuce. Claims of immoral civic embarrassment in Times Square were the cover used by Hizzoner and his phalanx of corporate boosters, who populated the neighborhood outside our church doors with shadows, muggings, whores, knife-wielding homeless crazies, welfare addicts, and broke black males.

When the sidewalks were cleansed of the "characters" who supposedly unnerved the tourists, the big Broadway houses were cleansed as well. No one caught on that the theater indoors was related to the theater outdoors. They went vanilla together, and though "Broadway is dead!" had been screamed like Ethel Merman for many years, the real death, when it came, was sudden and unmistakable. By 1998, whichever direction you walked, from Drama Books south, or from Joe Allen's east, or the International Center of Photography west, or the Port Authority north, there wasn't a thing of substance to stop you and force a personal question. You could really work on your tourist drift, your bovine browsing, your "nice time."

The streets evolved into the hallways of a mall, overpoliced, oversurveilled, and bland with visitors from outer Paramus. This could be called Consumer Theater, whose leading actors perform on the shoulders of Diane Sawyer or Bryant Gumbel, while those in the chorus jump up and down waving to their grandmothers in Dubuque. You couldn't have in that shot, for example, a middle-aged black man monologuing to no particular audience. Arrest those characters before they get in the frame—that was the point.

Now the lights of Broadway shine for shows that are nothing but long commercial breaks. They are movies adapted to the stage, mostly. These are merchandising vehicles that must never have the qualities of a well-told story because such a thing would compete with the selling of the products. A really powerful story is not easily controlled as it passes into the rapt audience. A real story must have in it, usually at about the two-thirds point in the narrative, *the Unknown*.

We're all aware of the feeling of weightlessness that a great story floats us up into. We can't know the ending, the fates of people onstage are at risk; they can mutate, suffer, fly away, even decisively change our lives as we sit there. This unknowable plot point has been stuffed with dazzling/distracting special effects in Disney films and plays—it certainly is in *The Lion King*. In New York's Times Square, the same can be said for the theater of the sidewalks—now there is nothing to fear, since any person with an unknowable quality in their "story" will soon lose their freedom and possibly their rights as a citizen.

Once the writer Walter Benjamin described the obsolescence of human experience after World War I, when the individual faced no-man's-land, where everything was bombed and strafed and burned. Only the clouds above could be remembered as having originated from life on earth. Times Square after Giuliani sells the same apocalyptic idea—here is life's destruction cheerfully displayed, where cultural change is outlawed because the arts are powerless. Here is the international village common, where once two hundred original dramas opened each season, become a Vegas-like mall.

Broadway is a single show now. It's called *Consumed!* The critics love it. Here's the plot: Life is dramatized as nothing but a commercial break between the unknown before you're born and the death after you've spent it all.

★   ★   ★

The first thought I had when I sank into the lipsticky chair of a thousand parties was: I came to Broadway thinking this was the Mecca of my art form, and it's devolved into the annual revival of a single play by Arthur Miller. Let me sit in this empty, dark theater and start over. I'm not saying I was an especially tragic figure. Everyone in this culture of consumerism is negotiating with the sneaky feeling that real life is more interesting than life becomes after you fall for the advertising.

I started to look forward to the dark hours, at 3 a.m., at 4 a.m., when the stained-glass windows would begin to glow. I would open my eyes and seamlessly enter the dream of the room. Very faintly at first, backlit by the all-night Mickey smile of the Great White Way three avenues to the east, I'd see the lamb of God floating across the dark pews. The petrified images drifted over me, coming to life, pushed by the seething light of that imperial consumerism. There were the doves of peace, and the angels themselves, luminously hovering in my hushed hologram.

And now, in this hallucinatory predawn room, the domestic quarrels heard through the air shaft became quadraphonic, and the fluttering wings of the pigeons in the open cracks at the top of the church could be thunderous. I would sit upright in my stinking chair and look around to see what play I was in.

In 1962 Reverend Sidney Lanier ripped St. Clement's traditional Christian altar down, just as Reverend Howard Moody did at Judson Memorial Church in the West Village, and Reverend J.C. Allen welcomed a feverish East Village into St. Mark's Church on Second Avenue. Each of the old churches was soon flooded with artists, happenings, serious readings, Robert Rauschenbergs and Yoko Onos and Amiri Barakas and Maria Irene Forneses and Dave Van Ronks and Edward Albees and the Berrigan brothers and, of course, Allen Ginsberg and his group of Beats, already elder statesmen, waiting by idling buses ready to depart for Freedom Summer.

Lanier had come to New York City in 1959 to join his cousin Thomas Lanier Williams, better known as Tennessee Williams, after having been a missionary in the Virgin Islands for a time. He appeared in Tom's doorway in his white linen suit and explained, in his orphaned-southern-gentleman way, that he was ready for New York. Tom started laughing.

Sidney took the job of second-rector at St. Thomas's on Fifth Avenue—a redoubt of Episcopalian WASPness on the wealthy Upper East Side. The church fathers knew nothing of Sidney's love of theater, and were unaware of his frequent visits to the back row at the Actors Studio, taking notes as the Method actors who would be movie stars staged their sense memories. The young minister's sermons in 1961 and 1962 bore this influence, drawing on his own interior revelations.

One evening thirty years later, in the library of his house in San Francisco, Sidney remembered in quiet detail one of his St. Thomas sermons, the one that lost him his coveted position at the altar. What he related can only be described as a total debacle. Perhaps we could refer to it as his calling, his exalted Oddness, his True Embarrassment.

That Sunday, Sidney had been invited to deliver the sermon. He gravely ascended to the pulpit and addressed the open face of the great Bible resting on the back of a gleaming sculptured eagle. The young cleric gazed out over a sea of bankers and industrialists and their wives. With Tennessee sitting there looking up at his cousin like a misbegotten waif in the midst of the hardened rich, Sidney began the reading of the Word. It was Mark, chapter eleven, where Jesus throws the money changers out of the temple. Sidney began slowly and found himself unwilling to look up over the pulpit's edge; he couldn't look into the eyes of the moneyed elite piously seated below him, their hands clasped over their perfect suits. He found himself unable to pronounce words that might be taken as an accusation. "And Jesus went into the temple and began to cast out them that sold and bought in the temple, and overthrew the . . . the . . ."

Sidney lost his place and skipped ahead to the twenty-third verse. "And Jesus said—Verily, verily I say unto you, whosoever say unto this mountain, Be thou removed, and be thou cast into the sea . . ."

When he looked up finally at the blueblooded WASPs, he found that he had begun an utterly mysterious sermon. In the Episcopal Church all fifty-two Sundays of the worship year are fixed in a great cycle of themes that peak at Christmas and Easter. But Sidney had, with the brownout that rolled across the pages before him, created a new synthesis. He'd gone straight from overthrowing the money changers' tables to casting mountains into the sea.

He cleared his throat and then came to full attention, erect in his purple and white robe. He looked at his sheaf of typed pages. His prepared sermon sat there on the eagle's back, but it would not fly.

Sidney smiled. "Well, Jesus is giving us courage here. What a blessing this is—we can throw out the money changers and we can throw mountains into the sea and so, children, what does this mean? Does it mean that we are free in God's eyes to change the interior decorating and at the same time free to move the holes at the golf course? But seriously, folks . . ." He was veering further and further from his prepared text. And then his eyes met, over the golden left shoulder of the eagle, the eyes of a king of industry who had just returned from Europe and found Sidney's collar in his wife's dressing room.

Sidney began to lift into the air like the glowing angels in the stained glass behind him. That is, he asked questions whose answers posed a risk to the entire social contract of St. Thomas's. In fact, he was now shouting in a church that had never raised its voice. "Why are we here, people? Indeed, what makes St. Thomas's Episcopal Church a church at all, with all these stone apostles and saints looking down upon us? Why a church? Why here? Why now? Isn't it on some basic level all *arbitrary*?

"What is it exactly that keeps us from making a choice right now? Right now, in 1962. Should we be turning this high holy place into, say, a bowling alley? We could do that if we wanted to. Wouldn't that be something, right here on Fifth Avenue? Or what about a skating rink with a big neon sign?"

It was at this point that Sidney felt the groundbreaking improvisatory forays of the Actors Studio rise within him and point him to the next thought (and if you're truly in character, whatever your next thought is, it's the right thought): "In fact, why is this the great and grand St. Thomas's of New York City? Must it be such an unapproachably nonpareil place for us to enter the kingdom of God? Why, think of this—if we were a few blocks to the west, we'd be in Times Square. The theater district. Then perhaps we'd be worshiping in a pool hall full of hustlers and unemployed Method actors and pimps!" Jesus Christ couldn't have said it better.

Sidney was called to the bishop's quarters that week and found himself banished to a new parish located in the darkness of Hell's Kitchen, a poor neighborhood adjacent to Times Square. And so he walked across the island and stood in the doorway of his new church, St. Clement's, and he asked himself this question: Who the hell is St. Clement?

Clement was a saint who had been martyred for asking foundation-shifting questions. Sidney had to muse on this a bit. The Romans asked Clement to humor them by praying underwater. This, it was explained, would be his new church. At St. Clement's the poor fellow is honored in a large oil painting. I can just make it out over there in the dark; it is a catastrophic example of its period—naive folk art by a faithful member of the flock, no doubt, a gift to the church. In this unconsciously comic painting of the pious man's last seconds, Clement is seen beseeching God from his knees on the river bottom, with a largemouth bass staring at him stupidly, as if the fish wants absolution.

Sidney soon discovered that fewer than ten people worshiped in St. Clement's and that some officials in the diocesan offices up at St. John the Divine wanted to rid themselves of the place entirely, to sell it. Sidney found the sexton that afternoon in a local Blarney Stone, drowning in drink like Clement and his sinning fish.

Soon Sidney was tearing away the altar of the empty church, painting the walls theater black, and discovering how to hang a grid for theater light fixtures in the vaulted ceiling-shape of a church. Sidney and his friends thought about the name their theater would have. They would stage the works of American writers, since not many had been produced so close to Broadway, only Eugene O'Neill. It would be a place to develop and experiment, and this would be valued as much as a play's completion. They called it American Place Theater, after Alfred Stieglitz's gallery of native experiments in photography. The first play produced was *The Old Glory*, adapted from the Melville story by Robert Lowell.

Tennessee wrote a play about his cousin Sidney, and it begins with a comic collapse, a version of the St. Thomas's sermon that ended with the pimps and actors. Sidney became Reverend T. Lawrence Shannon in *Night of the Iguana*, played on Broadway by Patrick O'Neal and in the movie by Richard Burton. In the sixties, Sidney wandered in and out of both the theater and later, down in Mexico, the John Huston film set, watching this send-up of, and homage to, his life.

In the opening scene of the film, Reverend Shannon climbs up to the suspended porchlike sermon room and looks down at his souls. He is unrealistically hopeful that they will see beyond his sensualist and aesthete self. When he begins to talk it's Burton's Shakespearean voice, and it's remarkably un-equal to the task of saying something that makes sense to his bewildered, squinting flock. The congregation in his small Georgia town looks up at him fiercely, condemning his latest local seduction, committed with one of the community's daughters while praying with her in his rectory.

Reverend Shannon preaches mellifluously for about a min-ute and then begins to break. He brandishes his good works, his family history, and they flow through him in a brash farce of a sermon. Burton is shouting now about his grandfathers and uncles who were bishops, and in the process he accomplishes something Reverend Lanier didn't quite manage in St. Thomas's—Shannon, raving, literally drives his flock from the church. Burton screams, *"You know. You know. You know what I have done! But is there anyone here who can say they have not sinned?"*

Shannon rises from the pulpit and descends upon the believers. The startled Sunday-go-to-churchers stand up, staring at him to keep him in sight, and each makes a turn for the door. John Huston cast very strange-looking people for his shocked Deep South parishioners. He gave them tortured-looking hair and impossible swan-swooping spectacles. The parishioners have evolved ugliness through idle and self-satisfied fundamentalism. Huston wants the old and the new clearly marked.

Their priest forces the parishioners down the center aisle and shouts them out into the world, out into the rain. Now, what is so very promising in this displacement? And why is this scene so beautiful? It is certainly funny, but there's something else, something vast just beneath the surface of the joke. There is a time when the church must be emptied to be filled. The unknown must flood in and drown everyone. The "believers" are so of that place, and Burton so misfits it, that all the characters can do is whirl around each other and blow out the door. The church empties and we know that the next thing to happen must be the world beginning again.

What a holding-your-breath moment, the opening scene in *Night of the Iguana*. I would mentally project the emptying of that church again and again, as if the darkness around my old red chair were a silver screen. It helped me think through how one might peform this emptying of our gone-bad institutions, now, forty years later. It would require the unknotting of a very harsh riddle. I kept seeing Reverend Shannon rising before his self-satisfied burghers and driving them from . . . I was going to say "driving the money changers from the temple."

I house-managed and walked Jessica and came back here to assume my position of strange sentience in the old red chair with the ribald stench, back to the empty stage. At a certain point, I don't know exactly when, sometime between leaving San Francisco and the onset of the Giuliani millennium, a band of rubberized, dazzlingly white canvas appeared in the unlit footlights of that stage: a priest's collar. It was sniffed and studied, as of course it should have been, by my small wolfish beast with the impossibly bushy looped tail. Jessica glanced at me and whisper-barked a comment, then settled down on the border between the stage and the audience and began her dreams of running.

The collar was size seventeen. Five dollars at the Duffy and Quinn religious supply store on Fifth Avenue, fifteen blocks downtown from St. Thomas's. The first time I went in there the old guy behind the counter said, "You look like an actor, so what's the play—*Mass Appeal*?" And I didn't know what to say, and then—"No, *Night of the Iguana*." He looked at the ceiling with that expression that people have when they are remembering something surprising, and then he said, "Well, well. Going for the old chestnuts, are we?"

So Sidney got me this job in his old church, the site of his triumphs. He lived at Gordon Rogoff's apartment in the west nineties for almost a year, in the slow process of depositing me here. While we walked around New York together, his memories tearing back the reflective modernist glass that sheathed midtown in his absence, he argued for this project, this character—a new kind of churchless minister. Sidney thought I should cast myself as a preacher who begins comically and then gets serious.

I retorted that, as a recovering Dutch Calvinist, I didn't even want to spoof a Christian. I treasured my trauma and would take it jealously into middle age. He countered with books by Elaine Pagels and John Dominic Crossan and reminded me that Jesus was never a Christian. Jesus had never preached in a church or a synagogue, either. It was hillsides, living rooms, bars, and the street. Sidney compared the "prophetic social commentator" Jesus to Lenny Bruce.

If I reflexively believed that Jesus was a businessman from Grand Rapids, Michigan, Sidney had me by the short hairs with Lenny Bruce. He makes me a smiling talker. I play his tapes all the time, for myself and for my classes. Be-As-Brave-As-Lenny is one of my most maddening mantras.

Sidney was throwing me out of my own church. Out of the church and into the street. Out of the theater and into the street. Then suddenly he was gone—back to the West Coast. He left me sitting on this empty stage, the pit that remained after his battle with the altar, left me with his idea. This new preacher proposal was very powerful, and I would be paralyzed by it or get up out of the chair.

I must have been sleeping again. Jessica is over there, not running in place anymore. She's barking at something, and then I see it.

The long white body is floating over the empty seats, staring from the cross. Which Christ is this? Some shape-shifter taken from the public space he was changing and forced to inhale metal or water. Now the bleached transnational wind finds a way into this crypt and throws Christ's body slowly over the silent, polished pews.

I'm afraid, but it's time to save my life. I have to shout now, and shout where these bones would shout, back toward the money changers. Oh, you are scaring the hell out of me. But I understand that the opposition has to be this basic. You are the congregation that smiles this light through the walls, and you are apparently huge. It is laughable to think that I can push back the tide of the great anthropomorphized mouse. But you are the impossible congregation that needs to be emptied from this church. How long have I been sitting here? Jessica, let's get some sleep. We know where we'll be preaching in the morning.

Jessica and I set out to study the preachers up and down Broadway. They were all over the map, some in shirtsleeves, some in the whole monkey suit. Korean Christians had pamphlets about the number 666 and the beast in Revelations. There was an extremely virginal Amish choir singing right next to the black Hebrews, huffing warriors in long felt dresses like a thirties Hollywood stab at the *Arabian Nights*. They were screaming that the devil was a member of the Masons.

Why do all belief systems come here to shout and sing? These sidewalk church people have about the same power as the old bones and haloes floating over the red chair. Don't they know they are standing in the reflection of the global mouse, transnational capital's preacher? The front of the Disney Store has a six-foot-tall version standing on a stage above the door, as if to lord it over the self-appointed holy rabble holding forth in the last little ribbon of public space.

And so I adjusted my sartorial presentation. I would be a southern guy, like the televangelists, but with just a touch of high church—thus the white tux coat from my catering days and the gleaming collar. And then I got my hair up like Conway Twitty.

I bought a portable pulpit from the Christian supply store on Forty-third. Instead of a Bible I had a black tape recorder, about the same size and weight as the great book. That took care of everything. Just feed the dog, put the pulpit over my shoulder, and walk to the spot. I kept trying to pretend it was an art project, like a task. I would be the only self-conscious preacher. In fact, I was terrified because I knew it wasn't art.

I found my spot across from the Disney Store, next to the entrance to the N and R trains, just uptown from the video arcade. I planted the pulpit like a square pillar, and I began. After a half hour of standing there like a religious mannikin with both hands gripping the pulpit and mouth half open, I started croaking something. The one piece of paper, my first sermon, had a pencil outline of Mickey Mouse, the three circles, the smile. Certainly my first shouts could not be heard or even deciphered. White noise poured out of my mouth.

I quickly backed down to talking as if someone was three feet away, the old monologue-with-no-listener trick, just to come down out of the fright. "Well, in my opinion, Mickey Mouse is the Antichrist. Yes, in the sense that he presents himself as powerless, the silly vaudevillian who knows he's silly, and yet by performing the American neurosis with the fearful, selfless smile, he is easily the most famous corporate logo in the world. Now that is a resurrection." Spoken to no one.

I may have had a thousand parishioners that first day, and they all had an ear in the middle of their face. I mean, I was talking to the side of people's heads a lot. Hell, I was talking into the air with no one around a lot. But this is a time-honored sidewalk preaching technique. I could see the real hellfire shouters in the middle distance, back in the electrocuted haze of Broadway. I could see what they were doing. They had that willingness to cast the sermon out there and let people walk into it.

But it was impressive how my verbs just had no action. "The only sin is tourism" and "Don't go into that sweatshop company store" could just as easily come out "The only sin is not tourism" and "Do go into that sweatshop company store." Having a personal value system at consumer ground zero is ridiculous on its face. I could have been shouting on an interstate in the middle of Utah.

And anyway, I was having grave problems with the Christys, Naomis, and Elles, and then of course Cindy with her lip mole. The Broadway sex workers who don't get arrested but rather get paid $10,000 an hour came down on me like erogenous zones the size of national parks. What do you do? The buildings seduced me with explicit demonstrations of sex I couldn't have.

All the eye contact I got those first few days was from supermodels who were six blocks away, but so huge that they seemed to be standing next to me life-size, talking about our weekend of champagne and deck necking in the Hamptons. I was discovering that resisting consumerism is a lot trickier than just appearing in a public space and telling people to stop shopping. I had to induce some sort of counteryoga to reverse the locked-down totalizing eros of sales.

★   ★   ★

If we ever have a revolution again, it will be against the killing fields of convenience. When I got out there on the curb and I was ready to empty the church of America, I started shouting, "Mickey Mouse is the Antichrist," and what was I? I was nothing because I wasn't inconvenient. Since Broadway became Vegas, the selling is twenty-four hours a day, and it's all the same products. Nothing about time is crucial, and you could be anyplace, so why say anything here, and why say it now?

Yes, if we ever have a revolution again, how will we know where and when to do the thing? Boston Harbor is too toxic for tea, the Winter Palace is a tourist haven, and the Berlin Wall is a Web site. And all the revolutions that ever happened are pixelated on PlayStation.

The early sidewalk sermons reflect this problem. I'm standing in the thickest vortex of corporate logos. The power is greater than any historical monarch, stronger than any villain with an army. But the power I want to speak truth to is completely amorphous. It pretends it isn't there while it controls your life. In these early tapes I hear myself grappling with this.

To sit here and listen to these neatly labeled cassettes today—my heart just reaches out to this guy. Thrashing in public. Looking for something. Flailing. The subject matter went from "Manhattan is now a Republican theme park" to "There is only one sin and that is *Tourism*," and always back to that mysterious focusing role of the passé rat, my anchoring evil.

After the first week, I was writing in my journal back in the red chair that the revolution will come from the inability of an individual to state an original belief, any single belief, ever again. I was dying from lack of voice. But I knew from my experience in the chair that you can't get out of this light, you can't escape the smile.

Here are some excerpts from those savage sermons in Times Square:

Hi there, little family, are you going shopping? . . . that utopian jolt at the point of your purchase, remember when that product smiles at you, you are actually at that point walking into the lake of fire! . . . Good afternoon . . . what? Well, I'm . . . no, I'm not ordained. I work for a church though, technically. . . . no, this, I bought the collar in a store . . .

Hell . . . what does the Hell of consumerism feel like? . . . mushy, a bit vague. Vagueness for eternity, no distinct political values, a drifting. [*Long pause; no one around, apparently. I'm trying to talk to myself—forcing myself to preach.*]That's Hell, when our opinions are all inside a larger opinion that we're not told about . . . don't you think? Don't you think that's eternal burning? Or, well, consumerism isn't really painful. That's the point. It's not burning, it's a nice little itching. A sort of minor pleasantness. You feel momentarily inaudible . . . you feel light and without responsibility. Like you caught up to life for just a moment . . . because you bought something? [*inaudible*] Is that all it takes? Buy something and life is solved for a moment? I don't think that does the trick, children.

The utopian jolt at the point of purchase! [*I glom on to favorite phrases and repeat them all afternoon. I'm in a river of people and figure no one returns.*] Beware the rancid discount of sin! The utopian jolt at the point of purchase! When that abdication takes place, when the devil excuses you to purchase that sweatshop product . . .

A person was standing nearby, about fifty feet away, pausing there—a woman. I turned to acknowledge her and dropped to a conversational tone. "Buying things. We say we will remember our trip to Broadway because we bought something. Is that the right way to remember something?"

And, she says "Lighten up, Reverend. I'm just buying a toy for my sister's kid."

Oops.

Through making notes when I returned to St. Clement's, I would try to remember the new theology I was improvising, gleaning the meaning from my shtick. Then I'd call it in to Sidney before returning to the sidewalk. I went back every day for a while, sometimes for six or eight hours at a stretch. Since the corner opposite from my spot at Seventh Avenue and Forty-second Street was an orgy of all things Disney, I would create elaborate prayers about Mickey Mouse and try to get passersby to kneel with me. It seemed like the only kneelers were Germans.

Our all-powerful Creator
You are the product become consciousness
How could I ever look away from your face
Your eyes always expanding, your ears are the world
Your nose waves above me like a black lightbulb
You of the swooning tuxedo, the three-fingered gloves

And the dancing yellow bubble feet
You focus our desire
And the power of our desire shines back out at us
Through your seventy-five-year-old smile
O Lord, we kneel in the Great White Way of your grin
All the crosses and moons and drummings
All the lost cities, all the gods who never got televised,
Know that you are the new God
Congress meets in special session to extend your
    copyright to one hundred years
They know in their hearts you are eternal
We are on our knees
America will not outlive the mouse! Amen! Amen!

This was a good method to bring people to a common ritual that was funny. But I wasn't satisfied with the mockery of the mouse; it felt like something *Saturday Night Live* could do—or are they owned by Disney? (Whether what I was doing could ever conceivably appear on *Saturday Night Live* was always a yardstick for lack of impact.)

After about a week I had a bullhorn, and we would hold town meetings discussing the new Times Square, with Mickey and Giuliani (his human counterpart) as the agents of this safe and unchanging world. Most of my own talk was about the death of theater; otherwise, I only had my own delicious traumas to draw on, especially abuse in the gaze of the Mount Rushmore–size blondes.

What I didn't appreciate at first was a given for veteran preachers: The air itself is written upon by preaching, and the phrases become corrected and themes that show promise are amplified as you return to the page that waits beyond the pulpit. In the third week I had a startling breakthrough, and I can hear on the tapes that I'm beginning to excitedly sing-talk, carrying higher notes for longer. The discovery: Corporations and their celebrity spokespersons operate very much the way churches do. This came straight from the battle of new light and old glassy flesh in those predawn windows above the red chair, but this was the first time it was clear enough to preach.

The most powerful church in the world is the Church of the Stupefied Consumer. This is a fundamentalist church run by famous televangelists. Recent leaders include Jerry Falwell, Michael Eisner, Thomas Friedman of the *New York Times*, Saddam Hussein, and David Knight from Nike. Children, we're in this church and we don't even know it! That's how fundamentalist it is . . . Oh, stop your shopping! Stop your shopping!

We are all suffering from extreme top-down enforcement by the powerful. This is the Church of Big Brother, whose religious rituals are distributed to us as prayers, objects, bad journalism, waiting in line for an hour, arbitrary demands on behavior. The consumer-believer is expected to fetishize a vast array of gadgets, pills, cars, rags, carbon monoxide, imagined embraces with celebrity lovers . . . it's endless. Don't you feel exhausted? If you don't feel tired, well, you're just cranked up on product love and you need a good swift confession.

The Church of the Final Consumption promises us, like all religions, a full, rich life—the trained actors who are paid to grin happily on the packages and flickering screens are sexily persuasive—but it turns out that the opposite is true. Products actually compete with real life. America's most famous product is the car. It is generally sold with the promise of sex with a rich, tall, thin, white woman. In fact, not since the '64 Corvette (with the possible exception of the '67 Olds Cutlass) has an automobile brought its passengers to a really memorable orgasm. The upwardly mobile orgasm, or "yuppiegasm," is promised by about thirty ads within eyeshot at Times Square . . . but it's not an orgasm worth gasping.

I was less afraid now, weaving words together more like preachers can. But the content—I was moving beyond mocking Mickey and starting to experiment with the shtick of presenting a reactionary costume with progressive text coming out of my mouth. Laurie Anderson said that artists have just three basic discoveries that they don't like to let out. Right-wing threads, left-wing mouth—those two are all three of mine.

Something was developing from being there watching people. Even while I preached I was studying thousands of shoppers. No performance is completely a performance; no matter what we are doing, we're a part of someone else's audience.

Shopping is the cornerstone of modern American life and this essence began to show itself, coming through the surface of regular dailiness. I had to stand there for months to see under the patterns. That lady had said, "I'm just buying a toy for my sister's kid," and her high ground of the ordinary stopped that sermon cold. But I began to suspect that shopping had a second underlying dance. The gestures of driving, parking, walking, taking escalators and elevators, browsing, standing in line, and on and on . . . they make up a formal dance, one that sustains everything in the world around it—service and security gestures and financial streams and architectural forms. The shopping became a kind of marching.

No one was just buying a toy. There was an elaborate but

highly constrictive series of stations of the cross, to which vast numbers of people were dedicated. They were shopping until long after the meaning of what they were doing had completely shifted.

And something in what I was doing would attract *facts*. People were plopping research about sweatshops and Disney on my pulpit. But they seemed uneasy about it. They would look at me quizzically, wondering about the right-wing costume. I would smile and gesture to them to come closer, and they would freeze. When I bellowed my best "Mickey Mouse is the Antichrist," they would take back their fact sheets and edge away nervously.

It had been many slow weeks since the woman said, "I'm just buying a toy for my sister's kid." It had been many unasked-for sermons in the anonymity of the street. Preaching back at all those pedestrians before me, I wanted to know this: If we broke out of this memorized succession of gestures, would we notice that the cost of these so-called purchases is precisely its opposite—giftlessness? Do we know that we are causing the loss of the same thing that we acquire? We have conjured an unintended world.

One night I was out there shouting "Mickey Mouse is the Antichrist!" Twenty or so people were hanging around listening. Hip-hop kids sitting on a car, slouching, trying to hear rhymes. Then this truly enormous pedestrian, huge like a sumo wrestler, of indeterminate background, started interrupting every once in a while, calling in from the right with "It isn't Mickey!"

Finally I got sick of my congregation's heads swiveling back and forth, so I invited the guy over to the pulpit. I was thinking, well, this is a very big guy, and does he really hate me or what? I was trying to read him. He says it isn't Mickey; all right, here's the mike.

As he approached I saw that behind him were a wife and two children, all in big sweatshirts and jeans. They looked like a little football team, the kids clamped tightly in place at the mother's side. They seemed afraid of the father, what he might do.

He started pounding the pulpit and shouting, "It isn't Mickey! It isn't Mickey! Why do you pick on that little mouse, anyway? Mickey Mouse makes my kids happy, and when I was a kid I remember liking him. Mickey Mouse isn't the Antichrist. It's . . . the Antichrist is . . . Barbie! That evil Barbie! That doll! She's the Antichrist. Barbie is the Antichrist! Barbie is the Antichrist!"

His wife was smiling; she was liking her man in that moment. She started walking over toward the entrance to the N and R trains, and my guest preacher caught her eye. I joined his church really quickly—"Barbie is the Antichrist," we all chanted. For some reason the young rebels liked this casting decision: "BARBIE, THE QUEEN OF THE DEVILS!" The baby gangstas stood up from where they were drooping and, now full of fire, kept chanting as our guest preacher headed toward his powerful woman in the underground.

TWO-MINUTE RADIO SERMON: SPONSORED GRANDMOTHER

We interrupt our regular programming for another moral advisory. I am Reverend Billy.

I was preaching outside the Times Square Disney Store—"Can't you see, children? We are suffering from consumer narcosis! We're turning into product-dizzy ghouls!"—when I was startled to see my grandmother walking up to me. She looked me in the eye and said, "I love you, Billy, brought to you by Nike sportswear."

"Oh, no!" I cried. "Grandma, you've been taken over—they've got you!"

And my grandmother patiently said, "Billy, we've had wonderful memories. I've watched you grow up from just knee-high, what a thing to watch, sponsored by your local Coca-Cola bottler. Billy, why don't you take a break from your preaching? Let's go have a sandwich, brought to you by Ralph Lauren Polo."

But I was sullen. "I'm so sorry, Grandma. I'm sorry that I don't have a sponsor. I haven't really grown up yet, I guess. My emotions are so . . . unendorsed. I'm working on it, though, Grandma. Will you give me some time?"

And she said, "Oh, I forgive you honey, I'll wait for you forever, and so will Toyota. Toyota—you've got what we want!"

This is Reverend Billy. God help me.

*The actor on the charged stage still known to a few
as the Times Square Disney Store.*

COURTESY OF MICHAEL SOFRONSKI / POLARIS

THREE

COUNTER VISIONS IN THE DISNEY STORE

It was the pre-Millennial time. It was the pre-WTO-in-Seattle time. And of course it was before 9/11. And so it was a time of innocence, of the happy Clinton con. In those days, the end of the world was a sort of hobby.

In Times Square all the preachers were shouting about the End Times. The tourists were amused by this; they would stop and smile at the New York characters who were hoisting themselves on the grappling hooks of their own delirious despair, waving the Bible like an ax. The upcoming apocalypse was, after all, a tourist event. It was an Inventory Clear-out Sale. There was a slew of it's-all-over movies: *Deep Impact, Independence Day, Godzilla.* And Mayor America was hawking the Times Square millennium as his personal prom.

I remember Reverend Billy then. These were the days after I'd started the "character" of Reverend Billy but didn't know if the role would become more than a strenuous arty irony. Looking back, I think of this period, in '98, as a dangerous transitional step in the early church. I was shouting "Stop shopping!" at the door of the Disney Store, screaming "Those Disney tchotchkes cause memory loss in defenseless kids!" at startled parents fresh from America. I was exciting the demons.

But I wasn't exciting myself. That's why those days and nights were increasingly fraught—I was releasing powerful forces around me, but I couldn't tell you much about them. One way to put it is that there was no church yet, no group of people with a name. I was shouting "Stop shopping and save your souls," but there was no Church of Stop Shopping. No one was reading their Godsightings to me. I was not a part of a revolution that resisted consumerism. I was shouting at the monsters that were leaning over me, but my comeback was a joke, not a manifesto. And I had no audience, just thousands of people with frowns, in profile. Oh, I hate that one-eared stare.

The sensory saturation tank of the new Times Square became less fascinating as the loneliness of it started threatening to inhabit the remainder of my life. I had always been in theater, usually in small experimental venues. Even in my old black-box days, there were some in the audience—relatives and friends mostly, ex-girlfriends and comped-in elders from the local nursing home who often snored during the plays' most delicate moments—who faced the stage, sitting in chairs. These old small-theater times seem luxuriant, in retrospect. Oh, for the chance to look out and see a face with two eyes . . .

My loneliness made me less uppity toward the consumer army around me. They were locked in their dance together. Maybe theirs was a kind of community after all. I came to appreciate that Americans buy things not just to belong to the product and friendly advertising cycle. They also shop to be together; they shop to belong.

Not that these musings changed my mind about anything fundamental. After I lost my voice shouting and put my pulpit on its side and sat on it and watched the dumbstruck consumers flow by, I didn't suddenly feel that such belonging excused buying sweatshop products together, or dropping bombs together, or idling in an SUV jam together. But I was feeling stranded out there, right-thinking but exhausted by loneliness. I was thinking about retiring from the ministry.

Now, looking back on it, I was slipping into shopping myself.

My relapse loomed because I was so sick of scolding tourists till the neon came on and the sun turned into litter. There's a relationship here with my reverse mentor, Jimmy Swaggart, who arena-rocks morals at fifteen thousand people and then afterward tries to find a fifty-year-old welfare mother to talk dirty to him under a sign that says "You Are Doomed!"

So I was ready to drift awhile. In August of '98 I journeyed west to an uncomfortable three-day family reunion in Michigan. This was my first trip out of Oz in five years.

Family. I'd lost my mother years before and lost much of the rest of my family in ways other than death. I'm not saying they aren't sweet people. But I couldn't remember my cousins' names. Maybe I was afraid that if I got to know these Calvinists, they might sic their DOUBLE predestination on me. Predestination is the concept they live by. It means that God, who resembles a Republican CEO, makes the decision about whether you're going to Eternal Hell *before you are even born*. Excuse me? Yes, my Calvinist relatives form a community by buying together, all right—the conspicuous consumption of eternal gnashing of teeth. And another thing: Born-agains golf too much.

On my way back from this family time I found myself

sitting upright in a bed in a motel by the Holland, Michigan, airport. I was working my way back to mere depression, if you know what I mean. I faced the prospect of flying to New York at six in the morning and going back to the sidewalks, but I was here holding my breath in this Lysol-blasted bed. I was tossed and turned by a wrestling match between two very jealous gods—New York City and my Calvinist familiars.

The Kills Bugs Dead bed was like a strong drug with no high. I was trying to be sensible. Of course this wasn't the time and place to make a momentous life decision—but I was thinking that maybe it was time to move on from the life of Reverend Billy. All artists are unsure whether they are a posterity-grade genius or just a posterior. Reverend Billy was an interesting phase—the self-conscious sidewalk preacher, yes, interesting. Now what?

I didn't have a television back in my little room in St. Clement's, and haven't had one since the '60s, so of course when I'm in a motel I switch channels all night. I'm the guy with the flickering orange-plaid drapes. Fueling my thumb on the remote was my lack of focus—not knowing what I'd do when I returned to New York. So jumping from Flexi-lizer ads to a Richard Widmark film to a soft-porn aerobics back to real-estate Ponzi schemes—this all felt good to my confusion.

Then suddenly, on C-Span, there was Jimmy Breslin. Breslin, the prototype of the workingman columnist, hair uncombed, voice gravelly. I dropped the remote. He was addressing students at Yale, and it was obvious to me that he was entirely uncomfortable there behind the ivy-covered walls. The mismatch of the man and the room became gradually hilarious. He looked like he badly wanted to be in his corner in a pub back in Carroll Gardens. He looked at his watch and trotted

COUNTER VISIONS IN THE DISNEY STORE

out the pre-stipulated Breslin color—how he had turned away from the grieving dignitaries at Jack Kennedy's funeral and interviewed the gravedigger, his most famous move, and then on to some stories from *The Gang That Couldn't Shoot Straight.*

He was rocking back and forth, working up the incantation of his own Breslin-ness, braying out the stories of the street for these children of privilege. Then Jimmy glanced hard at his watch and sighed with a smile, the smile of his old life coming back, for he had completed the job, filled up the allotted time, he was done. Somehow his speech had become long enough. Now it was time for the questions and answers. Jimmy knocked down a few.

Suddenly the podium mike boomed. "Times Square!"

The question was muffled off camera left, C-Span-like, but Jimmy's answer was in the big Irish woofer and tweeter. "Times Square! Do I approve of what has happened in Times Square?" He licked his old lips and let it out and brought those collegians up in their seats. By the end of his harangue I was standing on my bed screaming through the walls into the dreams of my neighbors, "Tell the truth, Jimmy!"

"Times Square used to be the place where stories started. A guy stands right there in his life with a couple bucks and an idea to get a couple more, walking around looking for a way in. What do you call that? That's a story waiting to happen. You got people wearing clothes that you can barely look at, and when you do look at them you burst out laughing, and when you're done laughing their hand is disappearing from your pocket and you'll find out about it later. You want a story, kids? You hire me to come up here to Yale to tell you how to make a story? Go to Times Square and stay there until the story pushes you up against a wall. That's where the stories are!"

"Preach it, Reverend Jimmy!"

He was pounding the podium, and the podium became a pulpit. And then he lit into Rudy Giuliani. It was more than a scathing attack, it was nothing less than the identification of evil where no one was noticing it, the explanation of evil in a time when our concept of it has atrophied to a discount apocalypse. As for me, this was a sermon I could ride; I felt future years of solid faith coming with each tirading minute.

I got on the jet ready for some serious shouting down in the streets. St. Jimmy sent me back into the fluorescent candy wrappers rolling across my altar, sent me back to the mouse who smiles like the mayor, the mouse with the implacable face that turns the stories caught in its gaze to dust.

The Breslin C-Span revelation returned me to Times Square. But I was still drifting.

I found myself reciting the script of my psychodrama. A walk in Times Square was still, for me, a personal confrontation with the seventy-foot-long Christy Turlington leaning over a coffee table at Forty-seventh and Broadway, wrapped around three buildings and gazing privately at me with her two oval lake-size eyes. I needed to turn away, but whenever I did I was carried along by walkers on all sides, streaming this way and that in their sharp hurry. I wanted to head west, away from Christy, but when I eventually reached the other side of Broadway, I was confronted by another four-story-high HAPPY WHITE WOMAN.

Each of the supermodels had a look for me, fresh with guilty pleasure. I don't know all their names anymore. Brazilian. French. They know they've got my number. Stella. Eva. Cindy and Christy and Claudia. Ana. Minki. Kate and Naomi. It's not easy when you're in Times Square and they all get you at once, a crowd of fifty-foot women, and I apparently did something really interesting with each of them. What would those very rarefied sins be? I was putting off preaching as I drifted along. Couldn't get my feet planted. I was pulled by the crowd-river into Christy's arms. This, in point of fact, is shopping. Now I was bobbing and gagging in the downtown direction.

I told myself this was the story I was looking for, though I doubted whether Mr. Breslin would agree. There comes a time when an uncle, such as myself, must think of his nieces in Michigan. I had been such an inconsiderate uncle. *Perhaps*, I thought, *I should buy them a gift, something from my life, so they would have a sense of what their uncle does with his time. A bit of the Reverend for my innocent nieces. My sister could refuse to sign for it if she felt it shouldn't be in Grand Rapids.*

And so, suddenly, I found myself in front of the Disney Store at Seventh Avenue and Forty-second Street. I didn't intend to shop there, of all places. But I shop so seldom that I ended up at the place where I had just preached for a year— that's where the stream deposited me. Sometimes you embrace an old evil like a lifelong friend that you've always hated.

The front of the Disney Store. There was something nice about not having my back to it for a change, shouting at the people going in. I walked toward it like an actual American.

The store facade was covered with thirty-four silhouettes of the famous three circles, the ears and the head of the irresistible rat. The doorknobs were stainless-steel Mickey heads, the windows had frosted glass faces, the carpet had the spiraling curves of his happy grin on a field of stars. I was falling into the logo world that I'd spent so much time railing against. I floated toward Pluto and Goofy and rows and rows of bright green Minnie Mouses dressed up as the Statue of Liberty.

I walked in and was held there with the others, the shoppers from the world, in the saturating fluorescent light. There was no shadow in that place. I felt like there wasn't even any shadow *under* things. The light was so strong it made people want to shut up. The polyester fabric was spun and stamped out of fossil ooze and then powered here from the jail-factories of rural China. The sound track reached back to the early mists of Disney's copyright control, "Someday My Prince Will Come," blending with the whispers of the cowed shoppers.

There were a couple dozen of us in the shop. Things were fierce but vague. The splintered remains of old Broadway were there, Disneyfied. The store was designed as a parody of an old theater with plastic theater lights, like big cannons, hanging from the ceiling. The sales help had "Cast Member" written across their T-shirts.

I leaned forward and walked down aisles of mean schizophrenic faces, the Goofys and Aladdins and Sleepys and Donalds. And then I was standing in front of Mickey Mouse himself, a four-foot-high stuffed felt version.

This was the one that stopped me: a Mickey who stared at me with the faith that he and I had some kind of understanding. The smile was amazing, really. He had the bubble grin of every snake-oil seller, every vaudevillian, every Las Vegas act, every bleached-teeth hawker who ever sold a trinket. If Mickey wasn't selling sex, maybe he was hawking time, as in Eternity. Maybe that was part of his power. Mickey is as old as my dad, nearing eighty.

Oh, no! I thought. *I've been caught in Mickey's eyes. How long have I been here? They're only circles of white felt—how could this possibly feel personal? Why am I looking back at the mouse? Oh, we're buddies now? Can I pay the price for this gaze?* The eyes and ears were too much. I moved to safer regions, taking refuge in the nose, which stood up obscenely in the middle of it all, like a blackened corn dog.

I knew that this mouse was actually a hundred thousand anonymous people in a corporate entity that has no individuals, only Michael Eisner, but I felt like asking those unseen citizens to petition CEO Eisner on my behalf. I knew the Disney Company was peeling my soul, and I begged silently, *Leave me something when you are through with me . . . leave me something. Let me go down into the subway with some stinking leavings from my old identity, a little fistful of steaming mulch from my old self . . . I'm not such a bad guy, just overly inquisitive about your evil machinations, that's all.*

Something happened when I looked into that exploded Mickey Mouse face, the nightmarish BUY ME face. I had intended to buy something, and now that something was Mickey himself. I would never tell the nieces that this was their uncle's devil. And as for myself, this was really just story research, just a bit of sin, so that I could better advise others to stay away.

And so, incredibly, I reached out my hand toward Mickey Mouse. My other hand went out, too, exactly in the gesture of lifting a little niece onto my lap. I was ready to take Mickey by the armpits and lift him toward the cash register. There was a line of shoppers there, each bearing at least one of these big-eyed Disney comic beasts in their arms. No one was talking. Everyone was overwhelmed by silence as these mythic creatures ate us alive.

My hands were hovering in front of Mickey's face. I remember something clicked and I held that position like a sleepwalker, my arms horizontal and my mouth slack. I traded glances with a woman to my left, another shopper. A new space opened between myself and the fabulous face, or perhaps I should say an old space opened up. I found I was having a kind of daydream . . . actually, it was Dad. I was having a Dadsighting. There he was, looking back at me, with his big ears and gleaming grin. And what were we doing in this dream? We were fishing.

Dad and me in a boat in northern Wisconsin. I was maybe eleven or twelve. We were floating on a very blue lake near Menomonie, and I wasn't watching my bobber anymore; I was studying the sparkles on the waves. The light would look like a face, and then like a leaping animal, and then like letters, like a message was on the water, and I would try to read it. In my youthful comic-book-inflamed mind I thought the lake was about to say something very wise to me, a message from a submerged world. I was waiting, wide-eyed, and then I turned and I saw—

Dad. He was groaning, I thought, but then I realized that no, it wasn't him, it was something else. He was pointing at the thing that was groaning. Three small jets were flying very low over the pine trees. "F-111s," he said. "Got a movable wing. Wings move back and forth. Climbs faster, banks better." I realized that Dad had a fish in his hand and in his other hand a fishhook. I knew what he was going to do. He would hook that little minnow in the side, behind the eye, and the hook would come out the other side.

Then Dad noticed that I was pulling a face. And he realized that this was a time to be a good father. He adjusted his sitting posture and looked down at me with a benevolent smile. The fish stayed in his hand, staring up at everything. Dad said, "There are many, many different kinds of people in the world, and they all want things. They all want the same things, and sometimes there isn't enough to go around. But the people who don't have as much as the other people, they get angry and sometimes they do bad things to get the things that you have. And you have to . . . you have to hook them sometimes—like I'm hooking this fish. That's life. It's why those jets are flying so fast. Billy, we wish that life was lollipops and roses, but sometimes there's such a thing as violence that is necessary. Necessary violence. That's right, Billy. Necessary violence."

Mickey's face appeared over the side of the boat. I jerked like a junkie coming to in the middle of a nod. I was suddenly aware that the woman to my left was gaping at me. "Are you all right?" she inquired. I defaulted to Reverend Billy—like advice: "Lady, get out of here, try to escape this place. Go back to La Jolla now." By the time I came to fully, she was already gone.

Mickey, however, was still there, staring into whatever day-dream, memory, or political action I was concocting. He waited patiently, with his trapezoids of glee. I felt a flash of anger run through me. I grabbed him, took him to the cash register, and bought him. Ninety-six bucks for the human-size mouse. I raised him over my head then and began to preach, the wrathful spirit sounding like a sonic boom in the store. I was using the same sidewalk theology, but now I was inside the wrong church, manhandling the dear sweet logo, having pulled him from the cross where he died of too much smiling.

The next thing I knew, I was being pushed toward the door by two police officers. I assured them that I had purchased the giant felt doll, and I had the receipt, but it didn't stop them.

They started walking me through the Disney Store in handcuffs, and a Dead Sea of disapproving mothers opened before me. This was the perp walk from Hell. It felt so bad—the embarrassment was of a totalizing nature. I had found my True Embarrassment. I was now in the smooth, suspended zone beyond the last moments of consensual clarity.

The cops put me in a cruiser at the corner of Forty-second and Seventh Avenue—a busy intersection, to say the least— and left me there as the crowds ogled. As I settled into the backseat behind the prison mesh I looked back toward the store and did a double take. There was the big doll I'd purchased, Mickey Mouse, inches from my chin, looking at me through the car window. It was as if he had followed me out of the store and was now smiling mightily at my predicament.

Then a cop's head popped up in the car window, smiling also. Oh, yes, he was the puppeteer who was holding the doll. The cop looked me in the eye; he was evidently a sadist. In his hands was my legitimately purchased Mickey Mouse toy, headed for some evidence locker, I supposed. The cop was a latter-day Charlie McCarthy, trying to make falsetto Mickey sounds while he tilted the great smiler's head this way and that. He kept nodding Mickey's face for a while, trying to be a ventriloquist, but I couldn't hear his voice for the din of the traffic. I could see him sneaking looks back to the audience of his laughing buddies in blue.

Then the cop opened the door, and I was momentarily afraid. Mickey was coming in first, with the cop's hand around his neck. The cop motioned me to show him my cuffs, and he loosened them, which felt better. It took me a moment to realize what he was really up to. He was handcuffing me to

Mickey Mouse. This demoted me, of course, to a cartoon character. But it elevated Mickey and obviously delighted him—his smile seemed even wider.

Witnesses outside were laughing, and some part of me wanted to join them in their merriment. I can laugh at myself sometimes. But not knowing whether there was a warrant out on me, not knowing if I would be signed out of the precinct house or have to go to the Tombs for the night, I was not in the mood for a joke. No, it wasn't funny. More like Evil.

And then I knew for sure that I was in the hands of the devil's little helpers. Some of the people who had come from the Disney Store were brandishing their receipts, as if to say, Na-na, na-na—we buy things and we get away with it! A couple of shoppers reached into their Disney bags and started following the cop's lead, puppeteering their toys like the officer had. He was glad to see that he'd started a new folk tradition, the taunting of trapped activists. His amused buddies in blue watched from the front of the store. The revenge of the consumers continued, with various purchases dancing on the hood of the car: a Pluto, an Aladdin, and a Beauty and the Beast set. I looked back into Mickey's face, and he was, as always, happy to be alive.

I suppose all of this was necessary violence.

Watching these events with a look that mixed open sympathy with hardened street smarts was a man I had come to know as Mr. Hakim—the proprietor of the hot dog and knish place on the other side of Forty-second Street. His grill fronted the street on the uptown side, from the lobby of the old Selwyn Theater. It had an open front that he rolled up and down, apparently oblivious of the risks in a neighborhood now described at the mayor's daily briefings as a panel from Hieronymus Bosch's most perfervid sketch of Hell.

Mr. Hakim had worked there with his family for twenty-eight years, and most of us in the neighborhood got to know his wife and kids, at least in that stoop/street sort of way, to say hi or trade a pleasantry or just to stand in that unstated mutual protection that Jane Jacobs calls "the cascade of eyes." The Hakims took turns at the counter. In recent years their business had shrunk as the all-night movie houses started pulling back their closing time from 4 a.m. and then 2 a.m. and then midnight. But that wasn't the real problem. Hakim's had the misfortune of being located directly across from Disney's stage production of *The Lion King*.

The Lion King, a middlebrow play that still manages to be inappropriate for children, couldn't have stood in starker contrast to what Mr. Hakim was doing across the street. Mr. Hakim gave people who walked up to him a dignity they hadn't earned. They hadn't paid. They were dirty. They were original. *The Lion King* is predictable down to its last puppet string, as most commercial enterprises must be. But Mr. Hakim had what in our church we would eventually call the Odd God of the Unknown. Street theater with real life and no puppets. Mr. H. braved death and brilliantly danced with it—the stuff of a well-told story.

One time, at three in the morning, I watched him deal with a guy named Dickie Boot, who was armed with a dangerous-looking knife. Mr. Hakim deflected him with good-natured banter: "Mr. Dickie Boot, if you cut me, I won't give you a falafel, that's for damn sure!" "Hey Maestro Dickie Boot, you're gonna scare perverts away, you know? Why don't you put that away?" And my favorite: "I'm about to come out there and kill you with a day-old almond crunch. Why? 'Cause you are ruining my Disney picture."

The night characters who haunted Giuliani's middle-class dreams, with their screams and bad breath, freely entered Hakim's stage, staggering into their pirouettes. Their speeches as they ordered their food became the script of a show that was directed by Mr. Hakim with a mix of stinginess, generosity, rope-a-doping humor, and rage. It had a life that *The Lion King* knew nothing about.

On the day that Hakim's finally closed, the family stood together behind the counter receiving the good-byes of the regulars. Among those most upset by its passing were policemen who joined the small crowd to talk wistfully about how many years they'd been coming by. The Hakims were forced out by Disney's lawyers. Their grill was destroyed and became a glass front like any dot-com office building on a suburban road in San Jose. The venerable Selwyn Theater became the American Airlines Theater, and the audience, consumers with frequent-flier miles to spend, watched Brian Bedford's interpretation of Molière with their mild faces. The theater's plays soon came to resemble television shows, starring actors familiar from commercials and sitcoms. Across the street *The Lion King* roared, but it was a commercial, toothless roar, lacking even one jot of the risk of an average night at Hakim's.

Two millennia ago among the Mediterranean cultures it was commonplace for unheralded writers to expand upon their favorite teacher's work. Today we would call it copyright infringement or plagiarism. But in those earlier times, a famous thinker's persona would be endlessly expanded by readers who competed to create the most convincing variations. Biblical scholars believe that much of what was attributed to the Richard Pryor of his time, Jesus of Nazareth, was actually written by admirers who imitated him in an exercise of sincerest flattery.

And so I'll have a go with St. Jimmy. St. Jimmy Breslin would have said, "Mr. Hakim's stage had lots of knife-dancing and playacting, bad words and worse smells, and maybe suburban kids shouldn't be there after dark. But the mouse and the lion across the street, pushed up into the lights by their hundreds of underpaid supporting actors, are completely safe, predictable, and pretty. At Hakim's it's dangerous to be stupid; across the street you have to be."

I still have the big mouse I bought. I never did give it to my nieces. He's sitting a few feet to my right, straddling my old Gateway 2000 monitor with his yellow feet and black spindly legs. And he's still happy, grinning as broadly and brightly as ever. His creators took my $96 somewhere far away, somewhere other than to the people who stuffed and sewed the doll. And I took him back into the Disney Store maybe fifty times over the next couple of years, carrying him over my head, in order to preach against his baleful influence on the world. I like to think it was a dance of which Mr. Hakim and St. Jimmy would have been proud.

THE CELL PHONE OPERA

For most of our actions in the Disney Store, we openly admitted to Disney security that we were not worshipers of the mouse. But during the intervention described below, we did not reveal our identity until late in the proceedings, the better to reveal Disney to its customers.

Pull on those stainless-steel Mickey Mouse doorknobs and it is like you are stepping into a tanning coffin full of smiling pom-poms. The first thing every pom face has in common is that each appears to be smiling with an air of assumed knowledge about your personal life. Snow White whispers to you about your virginity, Simba knows about your ambition, Donald Duck wants to help you with your earnest clumsiness . . .

You find yourself thanking these totemic polyester smilers for the life you lived. Your life events begin to reorganize to fit Disney's schedule; you induce a false childhood. Now you sincerely believe that Peter Pan mediated you out of your sandbox, that when the Little Mermaid walked on land you lost your cherry.

On the day of the action, about twenty of us headed down into our basement rehearsal studio, otherwise known as the New York subway. Our costumes were middle-class clothing—once we were in the store we needed to pass as customers for as long as possible.

As the subway creaked and plunged beneath the city, we handed out cell phones, fake ones that are available in toy stores for $4 each. Each of us would perform that night's in-store action by dramatizing a cell phone conversation. It was fun to rehearse for this type of action on the subway. There were a lot of straphangers on the train, and we practiced talking on our cell phones in front of them.

We asked our volunteer actors to imagine that they had promised to buy a gift for a daughter or son, a niece or nephew or godchild—a little one that they loved. That was easy, and soon everyone had a child firmly in mind. Next we told each actor that they were buying the gift for someone else to give to the child. We asked the actors to form a mental picture of this person. We suggested that the choice be someone with whom the actors had a particularly charged relationship, some- one they had argued with in the past, because the essence of this play required that each actor would change their mind about the errand and call their person back on the cell phone and argue that the gift selection was a mistake, a terrible mis- take.

Finally we concluded the third and final casting call. Each volunteer picked a Disney toy. To help in this, we read to our subway riders a list of Disney characters to be found in the store: Aladdin, Minnie Mouse, Pluto, Simba, Michael Eisner (via his autobiography), Donald Duck, Jiminy Cricket, Poca- hontas, Tarzan, Winnie the Pooh, the Seven Dwarfs, Mickey Mouse, Sleeping Beauty, the Little Mermaid, Tinkerbell.

The church deacons—you might call them political action managers—and myself went around asking folks whom they had cast in their threesome. We listened to scenarios like: "I am supposed to pick up a Beauty and the Beast coloring book for Christine, my niece, and my wife has me doing this on my way home. It's Christine's birthday." And then we asked this actor to consider possible reasons for a change of mind: "Beauty and the Beast is a vanilla-ized story stolen from the original creation by Jeanne-Marie Leprince de Beaumont. It is better experienced in the Cocteau film, which is wonderful for children and can be rented."

We paused in the sprawling Times Square station, gathering in a circle below the escalator that empties at the front of the Disney Store. We made sure everyone had their reason for not wanting to complete the errand. We asked the actors to practice out loud, and the station echoed with their cries: "I will not buy this for Danny! I'll tell you why!" "I won't get this sweat-shop tchotchke, Henry, I just won't!" The lines were already working as a political action, with passersby listening in.

Then we prayed: *"O Mystery Thing, be with these transgressive anticonsumerist actors. May they catch the ears of shoppers; may they find the sinning moment of purchase in nearby tourists and stop the buying with their holy-rolling Oddness. Give them the power to imagine their obstreperous relatives and the tenacity to defend those little tikes from Disney toxins. Amen."*

We went into the store in twos and threes, each searching out the shelf where his or her chosen devil toy was waiting. I walked in with a tourist wife from the cast, a raincoat covering my televangelist tux and a loose Rasta knit over my upswept Elvis coif.

On entering I found that many of the cast were already standing opposite the toy they were to betray. At this point I just wanted everyone to calm down, get a little more direc-tional, stop being terrified. The fact is, it was *very* charged in there. This was the most electric theater in town. The deacons were positioning themselves in prearranged visible spots. They were to conduct the Cell Phone Opera.

A few of the actors smiled as they faced their designated

Disney characters. I recognized that smile. Down in the train car, people generally had chosen a toy they didn't like. My "wife," for example, had picked Hercules, the dumb frat boy in the Catholic-girls'-school pleated skirt on the back of the flying horse. When she entered the store, she was confronted by so many aggressive dolls, clawing at her with unappeased grins, ready to Chuckie their way into her life, but Hercules was nowhere to be seen. She looked around the store forlornly. Suddenly she found the little idiot, deep in an unasked-for pumping-iron pose, facing the wall, back in the piles of sweatshop swimsuits. "There you are! Hello, Herc, little fella!" she couldn't help saying, and at that moment constructed a parallel of a child finding the toy it wants. Hence the smile, maybe just a bit rueful. This was good consumerist research, recognizing the reach and grasp of desire that drives the purchase.

The actors began to make calls on their cell phones. The deacons directed them to begin one at a time, so as not to arouse the suspicion of Disney security. The store manager was, in fact, beginning to think what an exceedingly good night it was turning out to be: Look at all these people! And so many are on cell phones. Actually, quite a few shoppers are calling home, see that? Everyone's got a cell phone nowadays. The head deacon slowly brought up the volume so that it began to compete with the industrial soundtrack of the store, Elton John on the floor-to-ceiling DiamondVision playing "Circle of Life" in the African outback overlapped with the goofy yapping of Dalmatians, probably a DVD release for Glenn Close and her bipolar puppies.

"Do you really believe that Tiffany is this stupid? An Eeyore fanny pack? Puh-leeze!" And from over the top of a tangle of vines with the geeky Disney Tarzan came this: "I believe that Simba the cub did kill his father, Grandmother! This is patricide, and I don't see why Carter should be exposed to such things at the age of five and a half! Do you want Carter to kill your son? Have you ever considered the consequences of toys?"

The deacons were cranking it up with the raised palms of conductors. Over by the Minnie Mouses in Statue of Liberty poses—about as many rows of the eye-hurting turquoise dolls as Nazis at Nuremberg—we had a consumer who was losing it: "This is not Pooka's idea of New York! This is not New York! Minnie Mouse with a torch! This is not New York! You want Pooka to remember New York . . ." Over to my right: "Jiminy Cricket is not Bobby Darin, okay? Listen, Uncle Mort, you have your preoccupation and you can go to Delray Beach with it, but children need another kind of MC, not Jiminy Cricket, not Bert Parks, not Mickey Mouse. Ask yourself why there's a fetish for toys in tuxes. You read the papers—you know where they sew these things." And "Snow White's waist should carry a warning from the Surgeon General. I don't want Christine to spend her life looking down at her midriff like I did when I lived in your house. . . .

A nice Brahmsian swell rose around the store, and it was not long before the manager realized something unusual was afoot. Plainclothes security approached members of our troupe, asking through clenched teeth, "Can I help you?" We were in the wonderful world of something's-wrong-but-what-exactly-would-that-be? The theme park had lost the cooperation of its animals. The deacons' arms were rising like Toscanini headed straight for the Schubert C-major: "I'm not such a political person, Aunt Martha, but if you don't want sweatshops, then don't rain that kind of indentured slavery down on little Audrey's head!"

By now the manager was smelling a rat, the wrong brand of rat. He was running up to people and saying, and this is a direct quote, "If you are not shopping, I can have you arrested." And of course "Chim Chim Cheree" was turned up to maximum volume—there's nothing like Julie Andrews at full shriek for quelling insubordination. The deacons were blurring now, asking for the peak performance moment.

And then the security people and the manager were surprised by a number of amateur singers walking slowly toward the deacons in front of the cash register. There they crowed with the voice-cracking conviction of people at home in their own showers, "I won't buy Pluto!" and "No, I refuse to buy these sweatshop monsters!" and "Our children will be free of this criminal big business" and "Eisner's billion dollars—I won't add to it!" and "Disney isn't supervising my life or the life of my children." The security people descended on each of them, but by now their collective joy made them unstoppable. Our opera stars sang without their cell phones, having dispensed with their fictional others. We hadn't coached them to do this. They were making it up, confronting the Disney Corporation head-on. That's when I got an idea: I would try to address Disney directly in my sermon.

With the manager ostentatiously calling the police and the cell phone opera stars still glowing from their last held notes, the show at the cash register was over, and the real customers gathered around in a curving crowd. I dropped my raincoat, tore off the mustache, and tossed the Rasta head bag. I looked up and saw yet another Disney character on a beam above the buying area, a surveillance camera. I stared directly into it.

"I want to speak to Disney executives who are watching this tape. Hello, gentlemen. We are here in the Disney Store on Times Square. I am Reverend Billy. We have performed inside your store; we have used it as our theater. And now we are coming up your wires; we are crossing the air on the electronic waves that you have broadcast over the skies. Sit tight. Don't panic. It's over. Yes, your actors are cutting their way out of their oversize Mickey and Minnie suits, the tourists are waking up out of their hypnotic trance, and the people who sew together your toys are rising toward your satellites from their sweatshop tables. Just wait—you will hear their voices."

Meanwhile, the deacons were hiding $10 microcassette tape recorders that we'd bought earlier on Canal Street among the piles of soft toys; we had a dozen of them with us. They had been prerecorded with quotes from Bangladeshi women who worked in one of the sweatshops that Disney contracts to. These devices were switched on as we left the store, and soon their plaintive messages could be heard, lamentations from deep within the mountains of tchotchkes:

"My name is Lisa Rahman. I'm nineteen years old and I live in Dhaka. My family is poor. I had to start working in the garment factories when I was ten years old. I wish I could go to school."

The security people started walking toward the voices.

"We work from eight in the morning until ten p.m. every night, seven days a week. If I ever doze off, the supervisor slaps me and yells, 'Why aren't you working?' "

From every aisle came the voices of the women who had made the products.

"My name is Nasrin Akther. For the last three years I have worked in the Shah Makhdum factory, where we sewed mostly Disney garments. I'm a senior sewing operator. My salary is one thousand seven hundred fifty taka a month—that comes to fourteen cents an hour."

The security guards were tossing the clothing into the air, trying to dig down to the source. . . .

"We have been meeting to make a union. This is because we cannot improve conditions. If I get sick, I have to spend a week's pay to see a doctor. We have no pay if we are sick. We have one day off a month. The work is so hot and long and hard that we do get sick. The bathrooms are filthy, the water is dirty. We suffer diarrhea."

trying to dig down to silence these voices. And when they found a recorder . . .

"My name is Mahamuda Akter. I work in the MNC factory in the Chittagong Export Processing Zone. We are forced to work to eleven o'clock or midnight many days, but the company always cheats on our overtime pay. They keep two sets of books—one to show Disney, the other one is the real one. We are being cheated out of three or four hours a day."

. . . they desperately hit the OFF button while customers watched them.

"When women reach thirty or thirty-five years of age they are too old and not fit to work, their eyesight is no good, they are forced to quit. They leave penniless, even if they plead."

Some of the recorders were well hidden, and the store employees looked like Keystone Kops as they scrambled to get at the words of the sweatshop women. But the comedy of the situation was quickly no longer funny.

"I am Sk Nazma, president of the Bangladesh Workers Solidarity Center. When we finally got our union organized at Shah Makhdum, Disney just disappeared. We want Disney to return its work to our factory. I hope for a better life for myself and for all the workers. If we could only earn four thousand five hundred taka a month, thirty cents an hour, we could live with a little dignity."

*This young man jumped from his bike at Astor Place,
interrupted our rally, and demanded to be blessed.*

FOUR:

NOT BUYING

So what happens when there are people in this church? What happens when a number of us stop shopping together?

Our parishioners, in the first weeks and months of not-buying, have started seeing the Odd God of the Unknown, or is she the Oddest Goddess? People send me e-mails reporting bizarre experiences in the first weeks and months of buying-lessness. We decided to call these reports Godsightings, after the phrase "Elvis-sightings." (A Godsighting is an Elvis-sighting without the Elvis, a Madonna-sighting without Madonna. A Godsighting is a Godsighting without the product.) In the Stop Shopping Church we hold in high regard those who experience Godsightings promiscuously, as in, you know, all the time. In our system, the Supreme Personality of Divine Godhead will go down that bumpy road of miraculously odd encounters. Could be *weird*. Amen.

After all, continuous gods are such a problem. I myself am a straight white male, and history shows that I'm the last person to trust with a continuous, enthroned God. After a month of the same God I'd start shouting at the neighbors. After six months my tank's in your front yard. So we went around sampling gods. It took a while, but finally we found the god-goddess of an Egyptian Gnostic sect who believed in a new god every day. They said, "I wake up and know that today I will duet with the mystery, and we will make God together." Yes, the portable, renewable Supreme Being. Sounds much safer. Although, speaking of bumpy weird roads, that Gnostic sect was butchered by the early proto-Catholics. Well, let's keep trying.

Before I offer examples of this post-religious vision called a Godsighting, children, let me make a few observations. First, I would like to emphasize that the shift in actual buying patterns among our parishioners, in many cases, was not really that radical. It's true that some Stop Shopping believers had to recover from years of daily trips to the mall. It's also true that others seemed to come alive politically, smiling as they strode with us into Starbucks and Disney Stores and Wal-Marts, interrupting the flow of sweatshop items with inspired foolishness. They found the embarrassing moment that is revelatory. They ascended to the state of Sanctified Oddness. They discovered a better America, a landscape of the imagination that became real.

But for many the shift was more subtle. For this second group of not-buyers, the utopian future that advertising promises with each purchase always was a bit of a joke. (When the seduction fails, it becomes silly very quickly. The tall rich white woman in the car bats her eyelashes, we say no, and she suddenly looks like Rodney Dangerfield.) Many of these not-buyers never consumed much anyway but now cultivate a new independence from the things they feel they are forced to buy, like computers and cell phones. Certainly many of us are over-connected and underexperienced.

Those of us who started this church didn't know that we would need this community not only to come down from the drug of that great antidepressant shopping, but also to confess to one another our Godsightings.

The gathering together of our church dates more or less from the Seattle-WTO winter of '99-'00, when public-space bravery became inspiring again. (The lady who purchased the turtle costumes for the activists who famously blocked the front lobby of the WTO delegates' hotel also bought robes for the Stop Shopping Gospel Choir.) These anti-globalization theatrics created an expectation that we would return to our neighborhoods with a new readiness to defend community gardens and local businesses against transnational capital. Going all the way from the macro to the individual, the readiness to regulate one's own consumption is ultimately private. There is an economy in the interior of a person. We needed to find a new kind of vivid privacy.

A new kind of privacy? Ironically, that is what made it necessary to support each other in a church, a community, when we returned from our private lives. We had to help each other with the Godsightings: the carnival of memories, so surprising we described them as highly produced, Technicolor with Sensurround, arriving in the brain with something like ferocity. (Using movie words to describe these visions doesn't seem quite right; these are late-stage-capitalism entertainment terms, stand-ins for our own words, which we will invent and apply in due time. As Jello Biafra says, we must BECOME THE MEDIA.) We used our Godsightings as replacements for product visions such as advertising, Hollywood, fashion. We apparently had always had these broadcastings, waiting in our bodies. They were our chosen stories.

Godsightings can become very clear and return again and again, like daydreams. They can be so strong that they stop you and demand that you recognize your identity. Godsightings change your face. You become your extreme self. After all, not participating in the commodified life can be a full-time job. You might get flooded with unexpected codes of intelligence, whole stories like memories from the future with secret beatings of drums, logic systems that float around in the dark looking for an argument, beauty, patterns of cooperation in elements that were thought to be chaotic, talking tattoos, laughing fits, and visions of Peace.

The shopping gods try to tell us that there would be no world without products, no economy, no sex, and nothing to do. In this way they have persuaded *us* to give up on the control of our lives and the direction of our country. Do we believe in product life so much that we can never change?

And now a reading of the Word from the Book of Thomas, evicted from the New Testament by the male honchos in the Palestine Screenwriters Guild. This is a quote from Mary Magdalen's star monologuist, the Andy Kaufman of his time, Jesus of Nazareth.

If you bring forth that which is within you, that which you bring forth will save you.
If you do not bring forth that which is within you, that which you do not bring forth will destroy you.

If the use of the word "you" by Jesus and Mary here refers to individual human beings then they anticipated Freud by two thousand years. But it's more interesting to extend the meaning of "you" to groups, families, towns, nation-states, the species, the earth.

The product-centered life, we now believe, keeps the stuff stuffed, the people quiet, and the edges of empire bleeding. The failure to bring forth on the national stage leaves us with the current paucity of political ideas; there is just no imagination at work. Perhaps you are old-fashioned enough to think that the arts should be our font of imagination. Well, there won't be any collective bringing forth if stages and museums have lost public funding and are stranded with nothing but the sponsorship of Philip Morris.

We have another twist on Christ's lesson. The way I've always seen the two sentences translated, the bringing forth comes from within. Our Godsightings seem to come from within and from outside simultaneously. Ultimately you can't pinpoint where many of the stories come from. Some are undoubtedly chosen stories from the core. Some are dreams or memories, but a dream that is remembered becomes joined to the thing from the outside that flushed it out, or tripped the recall, and is immediately given a specific life—it becomes the language that describes it.

Important point: The outside world brings this bringing forth as much as the individual brings it. And so we are vulnerable. Our Godseeing—imagination needs political protection from the control of the outside world, which surveils it, advertises it, car-jams it, and covers it in a sea of identical details. The outside from which we bring forth the things that will save us must be free. A healthy swamp, not a mall, keeps our freedom to imagine. A Main Street does, yes, and a Wal-Mart doesn't. A good song does, a war, no.

And following the withdrawal of the product fetish, God-sightings come from both inside and outside with unexpected quickness, the way that a river seems to multiply with life so soon after the pollution is stopped.

We offer below some examples of Godsightings from folks who have been buying less. I hope these sightings encourage others to bring forth themselves. And let's stay in touch, because this whole enterprise is unpatriotic, bad for bad jobs, bad for the Bushes, and illegal.

Note: These believers gave permission to reprint what appears here, but many sightings cannot and should not be shared. We don't subscribe to the world of frenetic confession. There are more Godsightings posted at the church Web site, Revbilly.com, and we invite you to send details of any sighting with your first name and the place on the earth where it came up.

Dear Reverend,

I wandered into an old junk shop and found a huge man there painting tiny little figurines of great Indian chiefs. It was impossible to believe a man that big could be past eighty. But he was. He had been a trucker before the interstates and told me all about how much more of life you saw when you drove right through every town. He told me he had something amazing to show me and I followed him out to his ranch—he led me to a huge old airplane hangar and we walked inside. The two ends of the hangar were hung with nets and there were thousands of songbirds everywhere, singing thousands of songs, and I stood and watched them flicker all around him. He reached out his enormous hand and a tiny little yellow-breasted bird landed right on the tip of his finger.

Sabrina, Garnerville, NY

I have a sighting. I was in a public building where lots of people sit in chairs and wait for their number—that kind of place. I was sitting behind a man in a blue windbreaker. He was angled so he was looking up at a large window and I was looking at the round big shape of his back. He was in his fifties, and he was holding a cap in his hands. There was a polite feeling from him, sitting there so still, holding his hat. I was looking at him, at his back and the back of his head, for a long time and—why? Then I knew exactly because I had a very strong feeling. It was of sorrow, very deep loss. I think he lost his child or he lost the love of his life and it was so hard for him right now. I got all of this from the feeling that was streaming from him, from every part of him. I stood up and walked around him in front of the window and he looked up at me without asking any questions. He knew why I was looking into his eyes and he knew that his feeling was in me too. I put my hand on his shoulder and he smiled that sorrowful smile and then we were both smiling like that.

Doreen, Santa Fe, NM

Well, I was minding my own business, driving down the New Jersey Turnpike, doing the speed limit, when I checked my rearview mirror before changing lanes and behold! There was the Lord smiling at me. She said, "Stay in this lane and get off at Exit 11." I followed her instructions and ended up finding my true love at a rest stop.

Susan, New York City

I saw this 4×4, a boxy-shaped car, on TV. It swam down a waterfall, somersaulted over a forest, and leapt up a cliff; it didn't seem to have a driver, this was the 4×4 itself doing all this. It was doing what a salmon does, then a monkey, then a mountain goat. It landed on a pinnacle of rock under an Arizona sunset. That was the dramatic helicopter shot. Then I turned and my mother was standing behind me. She has Alzheimer's. She was looking at me with a smile like the Cheshire cat. Down at her feet was a little circle of jars with the tops screwed off. They were different kinds of spreads, jelly, peanut butter. She arranged them in a circle and the tops were gone and we looked down at that and back at each other a couple times and then we started laughing so hard.

John, Illinois

I backed away from the product, or some of them, anyway. So I had this dream. Tell me what you think. I was watching an old Disney classic from the '40s, from back when Mickey Mouse's face looked different. And he was bouncing around the screen, happy like always. Then I woke up from the dream and realized that I really was at my pad and this stuff was on TV. What happened—I fell asleep and I was dreaming what I would've seen if I had my eyes on the TV. You following this? So I laughed and I sat up. Now I'm watching Mickey on TV and Mickey stops, he's standing in the middle of the screen staring at me, like he busted me. I'm feeling ashamed that I would ever want to leave him. He wants to be liked. He's standing there looking at me and he's not happy now. So I guess this isn't one of your Godsightings. But maybe when Mickey is acting jilted, then I'm getting closer to . . . something. Is that how it works?

Brad, Sebastopol, California

I remembered when I was about ten, I was at the neighbor's swimming pool, and there was this bead of water on the tile. The sun was making rainbows in it and I never saw this before. I watched that bead of water with all those colors for a long time, until a foot squashed it. It's my Aunt Joan, who's saying something up there, but then I saw another bead of water on her toenail, and that made me laugh. Her toes had lots of colors, in the sun, but she didn't know. Ever since, I always wait to see the colors when the sun shines on the water.

Louise, Camden, Maine

Social change will come when we value our own stories more than the media's special effects. If you follow a good Godsighting out to the end of its logic, you will find a pushing back of the empire of products. For instance, unemployment offices aren't supposed to receive the dead, and rest areas don't deliver lovers, and Alzheimer's isn't supposed to be fun, and you mustn't dream away Mickey Mouse. These Godsightings are outside commercialism. They have too much unknown. Each of them would eventually be illegal. But really, the thing about Godsightings that is full of strange change is that Godsightings make more Godsightings. The bright unclaimed space becomes vast with memories remembering memories, visions seeing visions. A writer from another century might call it "nature's increase."

And what if nature's increase doesn't seem to be increasing, as in no Godsightings seem to be forthcoming, as in an anticonsumerist's equivalent of writer's block? When in doubt, we go back into the store to find our True Embarrassment; we get our bearings by returning to the product and backing away from it. Godsightings pour out of the unclaimed space and, for all the phantasmagoria, give us a kind of direction.

Next, a Godsighting offering from the author.

Dear Reverend Reader,

I walked into a small shop, called Blessings, in County Monaghan, in Ireland. "Blessings" had religious items, lots of angels and jesuses, prayer cards, and cupid salt and pepper shakers—but also shiny bits of secular bric-a-brac. It wasn't a type of store, really, it was the personality of the owner, a woman who stood at the back with her big eyes. I stopped at a small yellowing book. The proprietor was, I felt, considering the book as well. I looked at it closely and remembered a whole time of my life, when we moved to northern Wisconsin. I was 8 or 9 years old, and we lived in a ranch house next to Curly Lambeau Field, home of the Packers. I was reading this book then, about a young warrior who left his home tribe to travel a great distance. It had a powerful pull on me. At this point I turned and looked into the face of the lady who owned "Blessings." I said, "I read this book when I was a boy. I gazed at the sketches of this wanderer, standing there in skins, looking out at the horizon." And she said, "And where did you read it? Were you alone?" I replied, "I refused to go out with my family on car trips. I would hide behind the couch in the living room, next to the wall, with the picture window above me, reading the book over and over." And she said, "Yes and did you finally come out from behind the couch, or are you still down in the corners?" and she laughed just a bit. I felt her generosity, and that she had every right to ask these questions. "I don't know," I said. "Take it. Read it again," she said. Then she added, "Tell me when you'll be rejoining us. Then you can buy something."

Bill, New York

I'd like to add a Godsighting that came to us through the Web site recently.

Rev,

I did the exercise where I back away from the product and run out and let something new come up. I brought a bag of Starbucks beans to the counter, then at the last minute I ran from the store. I wrote down the first thing that came up. Here it is: I'm thinking about flying. I'm flying with just my hands out In front of me. I "power" my flying by the belief that I will fly. When I start doubting that I can stay up, well then I fall back. *Believe!*

Benny, Ontario

THE READER WILL PLEASE KNEEL

The congregation will read the following words in a prayerful, soft-spoken way.

> Dear Lord,
> We can't believe that bombing is called security.
> We can't believe that monopoly is called democracy.
> We can't believe that gasoline prices are called foreign
>   policy.

The reader will please rise to a half-crouch, like an ape who has been watching reruns of *Friends* but upon whom a special anger is dawning:

> We can't believe that racism is called crime fighting!
> We can't believe that sweatshops are called efficiency!
> We can't believe that a mall is called the neighborhood!

The reader will now leave the church with an anger rising within that has the long-range implacability of a revolutionary. Now go to the office of a commercial politician (Hillary Clinton's office is over on Broadway just above Times Square) and shout the following words, while retaining a nonabusive solidarity with the receptionist:

> We can't believe that advertising is called free speech!
> We can't believe that love is called for sale!

We can't believe that you think there are two political
parties!
We can't believe that you repeat the word "democracy"
like it's a liturgical chant from a lost religion!

The reader will now drop this book and speak directly to the
president of the United States. How? Perhaps you could sky-
write over his parade. Or, whisper into the ear of his daughter
at Burning Man. Or—sew a small tape recorder into his pet
pillow.

George! Psst! Patriotism is not called shopping.
Got that? Patriotism is not called shopping.
Or better yet. George! Psst! This is God, George.
I AM NOT THE MARKET.

THE RAVEN AND THE WRECKING BALL

The campaign to save Poe House was the first time that I went to jail for a place. I wasn't shutting something down or demanding that the labor of a product be respected. I just wanted the old brick row house where Poe had written "The Raven" in 1845 to remain standing. This is what I would have done for Hakim's grill if I'd known better. By the summer of 2000 I had become aware of the relationship of places to imagination. We need to preserve the stages where we bring forth best. Poe was so gloriously Odd; he encouraged the personal visions that we would call Godsightings in our comic church.

Edgar Allan Poe's work, after all, stands like a cathedral of Godsightings in the middle of the nineteenth century. He loved the unknown. His characters would walk up to the line between life and death, cross into death, look back at life from within death, and then return (usually), ornately describing the impossible the whole way. Walt Whitman and Poe shared this love of death in life, although Walt came from the sunny side and Edgar Allan Poe from behind ancient dusty drapes.

The West Village citizens who tried to save Poe House wanted children to be able to go inside the place where he worked on "The Raven." The real-estate mogul who sought to destroy the house for a skyscraper, a fly-by-night outfit called New York University, argued that children could go to the Internet to study Poe. But it turns out that you have to have your body in it. This is like choosing a healthy swamp over a Wal-Mart, a song over a war. Hanging from your spine in front of a flickering screen doesn't do it. We need to pace back and forth where Edgar Allan Poe paced, peer out the window into the garden where the raven flew in, look down at the table where he wrote the bird's answer to his question: Nevermore!

Opposition to the second biggest owner of real estate in New York came from three fronts. First were the courts, where lawyers from the Historic Districts Council led the fight; then there were prominent individuals such as Lou Reed, Woody Allen, and E.L. Doctorow; and finally there were our readings of "The Raven" on Third Street in front of the house. By the fall of 2000 we were out there at noon several times a week, with students, community activists, and passersby. The poem itself had a power that prolonged the life of the house where it was written. The following is an account of an evening at the Tishman Auditorium, December sixteenth of that year, with the Church of Stop the Wrecking Ball.

I knew that it was not going to be your run-of-the-mill show. For a start, I had food poisoning. I was woozy from bowel-wringing spasms, and sweat poured from odd parts of my body. This is really fun, I thought as I peered out from behind the curtain at the auditorium. These folks, God bless 'em, had come to be entertained by a preacher, who was sick as Hell.

The head of security for the New School, the owner of

The Raven.

Once, upon a midnight dreary, while I pondered, weak and weary,
Over many a quaint and curious volume of forgotten lore —
While I nodded, nearly napping, suddenly there came a tapping,
As of some one gently rapping, rapping at my chamber door.
"'Tis some visiter," I muttered, "tapping at my chamber door —
        Only this and nothing more."

Ah, distinctly I remember it was in the bleak December,
And each separate dying ember wrought its ghost upon the floor.
Eagerly I wished the morrow;— vainly I had sought to borrow
From my books surcease of sorrow — sorrow for the lost Lenore —
For the rare and radiant maiden whom the angels name Lenore —
        Nameless here for evermore.

And the silken, sad, uncertain rustling of each purple curtain
Thrilled me, filled me with fantastic terrors never felt before;
So that now, to still the beating of my heart, I stood repeating
"'Tis some visiter entreating entrance at my chamber door —
Some late visiter entreating entrance at my chamber door;—
        This it is and nothing more."

Presently my soul grew stronger. Hesitating, then, no longer,
"Sir," said I, "or Madam, truly your forgiveness I implore;
But the fact is I was napping, and so gently you came rapping,
And so faintly you came tapping, tapping at my chamber door
That I scarce was sure I heard you" — here I opened wide the door;—
        Darkness there and nothing more.

Deep into that darkness peering, long I stood there, wondering, fearing,
Doubting, dreaming dreams no mortal ever dared to dream before;
But the silence was unbroken, and the stillness gave no token,
And the only word there spoken was the whispered word, "Lenore?"
This I whispered, and an echo murmured back the word "Lenore!" —
        Merely this and nothing more.

If the Poe House was saved, it was The Raven that saved it.

this grand room, was standing in the middle of the stage. I retreated to the wings. He addressed the mike. Maybe he had food poisoning, too—his impeded vowels were playing musical chairs. The word "fire" was pronounced nicely, though. He instructed us that should the auditorium burst into flames, we ought to stand and walk out the exits. Yes, we would be happy to do that.

I went back to the dressing room to do some breathing exercises, trying to get a feeling of traction amid the vagueness of this poisoning. Our producer entered the room and stood there, lost in thought. Then she said, "The cops are yelling at people outside, I mean, they are yelling at ticket holders, and, they are locking the doors, and, it's raining. But we're sneaking some in through a side door."

I couldn't believe this. The Tishman Auditorium is like the downtown Carnegie Hall. It has a wonderful history as the original home of the Actors Studio, the starting point in New York for Pescatore, Strasberg, Adler, Williams. Brecht would come here. These guerrillas were storming their own palace. I snuck out to the lobby—there was a circle of police from NYU, from the New School, and from Giuliani's City of New York, talking intently . . . about what? There had never been violence of any kind from the Poe protests. Was someting the raven said making them crazy?

It was clear that the drama taking place outside our theater indoors was in full swing. For the rest of the evening, the stage of the city and the stage of our play would mirror each other.

Inside, when the house lights finally went down, the choir was breathtaking. They tore into the first song. "Stop shopping! Stop shopping!" They were jumping. While I waited in the wings I realized that the energy was so high that I could float on it. And that's what I did. There was a this-is-it imperative in the air, intensified by the behavior of the police, the festive season, the spirit of Edgar Allan Poe.

Here was spectacle. A crack gospel singing group, twenty-five strong, dancing in perfect syncopation. I stood in the wings marveling at the performance. My mind wandered to what Edgar Allan might think of such a show. Had he ever written about his taste in music? I was thinking about the description of Usher's guitar music before his house fell. Then I looked up and realized I'd missed my entrance. The choir stared in my direction, waiting for their absentminded pastor.

I crossed from the wing into the light. Those first moments of the show reassured me, as they usually do. Audiences generally respond enthusiastically to the entrance of a white cracker televangelist, a Jimmy Swaggart for our times. But today I was missing something Brother Jimmy always has: energy. I jumped down off the front of the stage and almost collapsed on the front row. My deacons, my own pratfalling security force, looking like Men in Black but with Santa hats from a party store, caught me and steadied me. Suddenly I was seized with a need to be completely honest. I looked directly at the person whose hands I was clasping. "I need your help. I've been sick—I'm feeling faint and dehydrated. Shout 'Amen' a lot, okay?"

But I had a strategy for the food-poisoned pastor. Tonight I would play the eye of the storm. If the choir and band and deacons and audience were all going nuts, then I could just preside. I would move measuredly, above the fray, as if this was all inevitable. I'd be one of those older, calmer preachers, an Episcopalian who is guest-preaching in a Baptist inferno. Just be amused by the tumult around me, let people watch me watching them. This was my plan, although I knew that later, at the climax of the sermon, I would have to switch to a hot first-person present tense. The Spirit would have to move, and Edgar Allan Poe would have to help.

I was still down in the aisles with the deacons surrounding me. I touched a lot of hands and foreheads, and people smiled back awkwardly. Clearly none of them had been in a Pentecostal church recently. Then I heard Mother Dee Spencer, the conductor of the choir, shouting, "And now, ladies and gentlemen, the man who put the diss in Disney! The man who put the why in NYU . . ."

Wait a minute—I didn't write that. She made that up. I walked toward Dee. She was wearing a shimmering purple robe I'd never seen before, glasses, a wig, and a boa, and she was waving a voodoo wand. I started looking at the rest of the choir. Julie had her dreadlocks bound up like a bale of hay coming apart, Ruby had a forties-style church hat, Karen was wearing what looked like a small Christmas tree on her head. All twenty-five of my anarcho-gospelettes were beaming.

I couldn't remember my prepared remarks. But I rolled out the turtles from Seattle right away. Eisner and Giuliani jibes were good for jeers. And I had to go after James Twitchell, the academic apologist for Consumerism, whose name I'd seen in the reservations list. "Someone said that if you buy a Gap sweatshirt in Paris and a second person buys a Gap sweatshirt in San Diego, the two of you are in the same tribe, the same family. First of all children, that's—" Significant pause. "Bullshit!" That aroused six rim shots from the band, and I heard chuckles sweep through the five hundred congregants.

So we proceeded through the church service, which, like a real one, was organized in a succession of brief airtight compartments. First, our Fractured Vespers with the somber Anglican organ. Everyone embraces this part of the service. Regardless of class background or ethnicity, we all savor a moment of mock-serious Church of Episcopalianism.

Sometimes I look at our services this way: We're trying to rebuild belief. "Believing in something" is such a decimated idea, broken down by postmodern multiple viewpoints and by the co-optation of advertising.

The eye-of-the-storm idea was working. The food poisoning became a sweet slow motion. We did the Credit Card Exorcism: "I smell something deep, dark, and dank right here in your Sunday best! I do believe, children, that you have abscesses, pockets of sin—yes, I want you to take out your wallets! I feel the presence of credit cards! *You've been spending!* Now take out the cards and show me the magnetic stripe. I want to see a sea of waving cards. Deacons, you help these poor sinners," and we'd go from sinner to sinner acting out the demagnetizing of their credit cards.

Yes, the faux Pentecostals harangued them and brought God down like a great frying pan on these sweating consumers. There are times that this character is just flat-out fun. I was surrounded by New York ironists who were losing it.

One lady accepted my hand on the forehead but seemed truly disoriented by my intonement "You now have no credit at all!" She had a look of horror that said, "You're kidding, aren't you? You're not *serious!*" I had to keep moving, pushed by the deacons and the propulsive band, but I looked back at the lady and wondered if perhaps she thought she was in a real church. Or maybe she thought she wasn't and found out she was. And the choir sang its marching song, a great anthem: "We are in control! Mickey Mouse has let go of our balls! Now we can leave the shopping malls!"

Next came the Induction of the Saints, and our theme of the evening rose into the light. We were there to save Poe House from demolition. The place where Edgar Allan Poe finished "The Raven" 150 years ago. "We don't kill our saints first! We put them on our dashboards *before they die*!" And I invited Suzanne Dickerson to walk up from the front row to the altar. She had stood up against pressure in the community, agreeing to act as the movant in a lawsuit that got us a restraining order against NYU's demolition plans, so Poe House had remained standing through the summer. With that demolition stopped, we'd had the opening we needed to get organized. Suzanne was sainted for her work.

Our next canonization was of Michael Deas, the Poe scholar who had countered the NYU disinformation campaign that claimed Poe barely lived in the house, that he had just flopped there for a few nights with a morphine hangover. St. Michael accepted his canonization and sparked cheers when he dared NYU to "have a soul." Then John Jurayj from the Save Poe House/Save Judson House Coalition invited us to march to the house after the show, where we would read "The Raven" aloud.

Things were rolling. I grasped the pulpit and looked into the crowd, counting on God or some facsimile thereof to save my ass. The sickness had curtailed any rehearsal. I had a sermon on paper in front of me, but I had long ago abandoned what I had written. As I stood there looking out, with the choir fanning themselves behind, I knew I was coming full circle. I flashed back to the Times Square sidewalks, back to basic, raw street preaching, back to trusting the great unknown.

The first part of the Tishman sermon was simply a conjuring up of Poe. His house was only nine blocks downtown, and I could easily ask the audience to imagine Edgar Allan Poe just outside, taking a walk on Sixth Avenue. With "The Raven," Poe became an instant pop star of his time. In 1845 everyone was quoting that pagan spokesbird. For Poe, who until then had lived in complete obscurity, walking down the street must have become a very different experience. I asked my flock at Tishman to imagine shouting at him as he strolled by in his old but impeccably maintained coat, "Nevermore, Eddie! Fuhgeddaboudit!" The congregation practiced: "Nevermore, Eddie! Fuhgeddaboudit!" We were inviting him to spend time with us by employing this traditional New Yorker's abusive compliment. If we were going to raise the writer from the dead, we had to remind him of when his life was fun.

The impromptu sermon was working. I was repeating a single phrase five times and a congregation of ironists was shouting "Amen" back, a knowing response that contained both parody and the hope that we would soon transcend it. With this sort of spontaneous preaching you have to play the silences between the phrases with power, because you're waiting for the current thought to provide the next. Everyone knows it, and that creates drama. So Tishman Auditorium had become one curved collective mind, waiting for the next thought.

I was in a curious state of nausea and ecstasy. The stage felt wobbly, like liquid under my feet, a seashore. Now I was balancing on that edge, thinking of the scene in *The Red Shoes* where the audience becomes an ocean. I wanted to fall into it and float there for a while.

Children, let me ask you a question. Think about this question: Do you ever want to be resurrected? Ever want to rise from the slab? The difficult thing about rising from the dead is you have to realize that you are dead first, and for a moment actually forget life.

Edgar Allan Poe walked slowly toward the line of death, and then crossed it, risked everything, and then crossed back toward life from behind death and he didn't hurry. He savored, he studied that crossing. He let the raven be implacable. He didn't lie to himself. He didn't bribe death! He didn't make a deal! He wasn't writing ad copy. Near death he found the whole world of unconscious life. It must have been terrible! But oh, what a gift! Thank you, Edgar Allan Poe! Let's hear somebody be grateful tonight! Thank you! Thank you! Edgar Allan Poe! Amen! Amen!

Children, I read Poe last summer, "MS. Found in a Bottle," "The Murders in the Rue Morgue," "William Wilson," "The Cask of Amontillado," story after story. And I found myself wanting to be resurrected. Looking back—I want to confess, children—I didn't just want to save Poe House. I was looking for my own light that I believed was waiting for me just beyond a wall, a lid, a cover—that I felt was always

there—somewhere—in the city. So I became a wor-
shiper in the Church of Poe! I became a character myself. Or rather, I became what I think Poe would've
wanted had he written about a sidewalk preacher.

So I was calling for NYU to stop the demolition.
But I was also setting up my portable pulpit on grat-
ings, in construction sites, near cracks in walls where
the earth comes through. Poe-type places. I'm preaching in the Gothic corner of the park, shouting where
the bones are supposed to be, under the moon, taking
the pulpit on the rooftop of a Catholic church. That
was a good Poe moment, I thought, and I never ask
for a permit. And so I went to the Tombs. Through
September and October and November I'd be led away
to the Tombs, where Eddie would have wanted me to
go if I were one of his characters. Wouldn't he want
me to set up my pulpit in his darkness, and find the
secret places, the seam in the landscape where the earth
pours out, the changings of New York, where the line
between death and life is nearby?

And then one day, children, I found an old key to
a back door of Judson Church in my desk. I called
around, and about twenty-five of us snuck into the
construction site at the rear of the church with a ladder
and ropes and signs and musical instruments. And we
climbed up onto the scaffolding that encircles Poe
House and we read "The Raven" to the people on
Third Street below us. They stopped to listen to our
voices rising from the old house, ghosts in full voice.
Tony Torn was dressed up like a raven, and he read the

whole poem from a long scroll, with the raven's beak jutting from his forehead. He dedicated the reading to his mother, Geraldine Page, a distant relative of our author. We had a band up there on the scaffolding—a saxophone, and a keyboard, and a French horn. We led the crowd below in chants. The obvious one: "Tear down Poe House? NYU: Nevermore!"

Soon the police closed off the street. They made their way through the old Judson House to the scaffolding and they climbed up and arrested me. They arrested me for reading "The Raven" at Poe's house! Think about that. They arrested me at the very spot where he made his final revisions and gathered together the other poems in the collection. We are an echo of his scrawling quill, 150 years in the future—and they arrest us!

When did it get this conservative? When was it impossible for something to be just the right thing? The action standing alone, without sponsorship, without the corporate frame—simply the right thing. I'm reading "The Raven" where he wrote it, to honor him, and to save the memory of his writing it, and all they can think to do is to cuff me and take me to the Tombs. Sometimes violence is simply an absence of imagination.

So now I'm in the police cells at 100 Centre Street and I'm led down the puke-green hallways in a line with the others. Cops are telling us to stop and start, and face the wall and turn around. And I'm in the terror now, children. The line of death is nearby. The noble political action on the scaffolding outside the great man's window is a long way away. I'm walking bowed over, the way you do when you're cuffed. And I see a little office in the maze and it makes my heart sink. They have such old computers, from sometime in the 1980s. Pre-junk-bond-era computers, the sort you'd play Pac-Man or Pong on, the sort that could take a long time to process your record so that you disappear forever. I'm in the Tombs.

I'm shunted into the forty-person cell with people slumped in corners who have been here for days and don't know why. Their posture resembles driftwood. Cockroaches run up and down the walls, busy busy busy. Young men of color as far as the eye can see, sleeping at angles, or pleading with a cousin on the phone down to their last quarter, then sinking back on the floor to find somewhere to sleep, resting their head on someone's shin, the floor covered with men.

I'm doing a bit from every Poe story, tracing the shape of Poe's trope down and behind death. But now that I'm here and have the opportunity to look back at life from this side, as Poe repeatedly instructed us to do, now I'm wondering, how will this save Poe House? NYU won the court case. They can get their demolition permit anytime they want to. It costs many thousands of dollars every day they wait. Inevitably Third Street will lose the old three-story buildings and a 169-foot-tall law school tower will go up in their place, as high as a seventeen-story apartment building, with its shadow reaching across the park all the way to the Washington Arch. What makes me think that won't happen? No one has ever stopped NYU.

Why am I insisting on being a Poe character? Is this the beautiful terror of death or am I just willfully doing time in this apartheid pit? Have I been miserable and bowing to my equally miserable audience friends like a seventies performance artist, inflaming some personal need and calling it art? Think carefully. Once you get past the vaguely interesting presentational surface of "acting like a Poe character" from 150 years into Poe's future, well, what, really, can come from mimicking his downwardly mobile but self-aware freaks?

I'm in the Tombs, children, standing there in my priest's collar, wide awake and full of thoughts. Jail is very powerful. Entrapment. That's part of Poe's power. We see the pendulum blade come down, feel the pit nearby. We are fully conscious when our well-meaning weeping relatives bury us. If we don't succumb to hopelessness, then we will never have resurrection. Poe characters always forget that Poe is writing them; when they are freed from premature burial they are grandly, almost comically surprised. But there I go again. In fact, I'm not a Poe character. What am I? Who am I? They've lost my file. Every time the cop reads out the list of names for arraignment, I'm not on it. And there are guys going free who haven't been here for nearly as long as me.

It's 2 a.m. It's 4 a.m. The hourly lists of names don't mention me. I'm trying to do a Zen slowdown, but waves of anguish ruin it.

Dear Edgar Allan Poe. What am I thinking? I'm haunting construction sites and church rooftops in 2000? I think I'm a Poe character walking loose in New York City? Edgar? You couldn't have expected anyone to mimic your characters. But did you? Did you walk all night confronting the Gothic demons of New York like Lorca did? Why am I mouthing the subtitles of your ghouls, your comically rattled actors? Why are we moved by you? Even Vincent Price couldn't destroy you. I'm in a tomb and I think I came here on purpose but I can't remember why.

A kid comes over and I wonder if I've been standing here with my mouth moving. I've been talking to Poe explicitly, a direct address in my jailhouse madness. I was looking into his eyes from that famous photo, the one with the slightly jarred mouth and the huge forehead. So how crazy am I? The kid is smiling at me mightily. "So you're a priest, huh? What are you doing in here, preacher?" I try to be polite but it feels arch. "We climbed up on the scaffolding that's in front of Poe House, where Edgar Allan Poe finished writing 'The Raven.' Big-money people want to tear it down. Do you know his work? Poe?" I can't make out his expression. He's certainly more interested than I expected. I'm trying to help him along. "You follow the Baltimore Ravens?" He says, "Shit, I know Eddie P." Then he shouts. It's 5 a.m. and he shouts, "Yo! Listen up! It's hip-hop from a million years ago!" And brothers throughout the pens start stirring. Christ.

Children, I will never forget this as long as I live.

He raised his arms and moved his hands side to side and said: "Once upON a MIDnight DREARy / While I PONdered WEAK and WEARY / OVer MANy a QUAINT and CURious VOLume OF forGOTten LORE . . ." He was rapping "The Raven."

This is a Christmas show, and so here's the miracle. He rapped out all eighteen stanzas of "The Raven." Or rather I think he did, because about halfway through I heard my name called out and the door opened and I was walking up out of the puke-green walled labyrinth toward the light. And I could hear him Nevermoring before the final door slammed and I was out. A perfect Poe ending. The despair was complete. I had tasted the Unknown. I had seen my Godsighting. And then Poe comes rising out of this kid, from such a self-made enthusiasm.

Now the chant "Save Poe House!" filled Tishman Auditorium, and the choir in their flapping robes raced into the aisles shouting, "Nevermore! Nevermore!" My job was done, and I looked out appreciatively at the singers dancing in the aisles and at the way the audience had become like a scene from a Brueghel festival, with people standing in groups, dancing, clapping, and singing along. I saw my sister Julie in the back row and walked back there and gave her a neck rub. I went and stood at the door and thanked the congregation for attending the service, as preachers do, and it all felt pretty good. We got our coats on and followed the purple madam of gospel funk, Mother Dee, as she wandered into the night air.

We followed the "Nevermores" out of the lobby, and there were cop cars, five or six of them, in full light-swirling alert, ready to start their sirens. We walked past them with the TV crews who were making documentaries that night, a Vancouver group of "culture-jammers," and the BBC. You always hope the media's presence will give the cops pause.

My memory of handing out glow sticks is a blur, as is marching down Fifth Avenue toward Washington Square Park. I was getting nods from certain informants, indicating that the show had gone well—people who had followed the preacher for years and knew a good show from a bad one. We chanted as we walked: "Hell, no! Poe won't go! Nevermo'!" and arrived at Washington Square Park, down in Henry James land.

We crossed the park and took Thompson down to Third, about three hundred of us, a good crowd for a cold, wet Saturday night. We waited for everyone to get around the corner and gather there. I welcomed those assembled and looked up at the building, up at the scaffolding where we had held forth three months before, where the band had played, Tony had intoned, and I was pulled from the pulpit. We all craned our necks up toward his windows, thanking Edgar Allan Poe for his brave work. I spoke of our hope that we would be able to bring our children up to Poe House and have that human-scale greatness in our neighborhood. Then we began reading the poem as the young prisoner in the Tombs had, as the gospel choir had, as each of us remembered it. These are words that stay with you.

I held the microphone of my little battery-operated speaker up to Donald Gallagher, one of the deep back-row voices of the choir. The "Nevermore" at the end of each stanza was delivered with great passion, clearly now being directed at the great corporation whose office towers loomed over us. The reading was insistently rhythmic, with heads bobbing to the beat and people at the center finishing at about the point that the people on the outside were beginning, so there was a gentle wave radiating outward and inward. It was an innocent reading, but delirious too, like a town meeting that became a ghost dance. We were from the Village, the neighborhood Duchamp declared its own nation in the 1920s at a famous picnic inside the crawl space at the top of the Washington Arch.

Many children were reading "The Raven" that night. And there were older Villagers too, people who had lived here for decades, who remember when buses waited on this very block, in front of Judson Church, to take people to Freedom Summer down in Selma and Birmingham—the days when crowds gathered in the Village for political change, from the Catholic Workers of Dorothy Day to the zany daring of ACT UP.

I looked up at the building we were trying to save and thought about Edgar Allan Poe writing his poem, trying to resolve for himself what death was, and what it would be like when his tubercular wife, Virginia, passed on. From his letters we know they had moved here because of the garden by the house and the park, which they thought would improve her health. He interrogated the talking bird about what his memories of Virginia would be.

Hundreds of Christian editors reprinted "The Raven" in 1845, despite the bird's declaration at the end of each stanza that heaven doesn't exist, because people were hungry for an honest report of how unknowable life is. The great dark secret that Christians whisper to themselves but seldom say out loud is that life is mostly unknown, can never be fully explained. Not by the Vatican, not by Disney, not by the Human Genome Project either. And that's why life is such a great story—it's a cliffhanger. The raven says, "You know what? Here's what we really know about death . . . it's Nevermore! But isn't life grand? You can ask me eighteen times!"

A police officer on my left asked for my sound device permit. I told him we'd be done with the poem in the next minute or two. I pointed to the house and told him Edgar Allan Poe had written this poem right there. Donald kept on leading the crowd in the rhythms and rhymes, pleading with the raven for a chance to meet Lenore in some heaven. The police were surrounding me now. I argued that we were not in the roadway. "Where is your ID?" the cop to my left said. I told him that I was in my performance costume, that someone else was holding it for me. And then I was shoved up against the car, my arms were pulled behind me, and I was cuffed and pushed into the backseat. I heard the crowd shouting, "Let him go! Let him go!" but it made no difference. I was headed back to the Tombs again.

Twenty-four hours later I was standing before the judge. My Legal Aid lawyer argued that I had already done my community service by acting to defend Poe House. I liked that idea, but the judge did not. I had to promise her that I would pick up litter for one day from Sara Roosevelt Park. Then I went home.

I slept for a long time, drifting back slowly from the food poisoning, the performance and march and reading, and prison. I slept and slept. Then I got up early Monday afternoon and slowly got dressed for the Historic Districts Council meeting at the neighborhood center on East Eleventh Street behind St. Mark's in the Bowery. Every couple of weeks the Save Poe House/Save Judson House Coalition gathered in the back room and David Goldfarb, the lead counsel who negotiates for us with NYU, gave us his report. And so he did again on that Monday. He told us that something remarkable had happened over the weekend: NYU had changed its position and was putting the issue of saving Poe House on the table in a completely new way.

The facade of Poe House was to be retained, and a Poe room, based on the existing structure and with its own separate entrance on Third Street, would be incorporated in the new NYU building. We were cautiously pleased by the plan, though we knew we would have to monitor NYU closely to make sure they did not renege on it.

Later that week I had a dream that I was walking with a child, holding her hand, a little girl, and that I took her to the Poe room and there was a first edition of *The Raven and Other Poems* on the table.

The NYU representatives who were standing among us that night as we read "The Raven" may have sensed that the Village was rising against them, as it most certainly was. They must have heard the jeering cheers when our newly created saints asked NYU to "have a soul." They may have felt the power of my fellow prisoner's rap. They perhaps thought twice as the gospel singers belted out "Nevermore" after "Nevermore."

But perhaps more than anything else, the reason that NYU couldn't just roll over us is that Poe's writing was deep within each of us. We had become a nightmare to NYU, like Poe characters clamoring toward the sunlight beyond the crypt.

It is usually hard to measure the effect of words or the impact of street theater. But on top of the litigation and the interventions of E.L. Doctorow and Jane Jacobs and the relatives of Stanford White (architect of Judson Church and the Washington Arch), perhaps that night at Judson Church was the final straw. Maybe we saved Poe House word by word that night of December sixteenth. Think about it: One hundred and fifty years later, the words of "The Raven" had saved at least part of the house where the poem's revisions finally ceased and Edgar Allan Poe sent off his poem with the great bird into an unknowable world.

I know that the end of our story is as romantic as Poe's hope to see Lenore again. Our much-fought-for agreement with New York University's squadron of lawyers calls for a reconstruction of Poe House within the larger structure. It's still possible it won't happen; I am troubled by that. A few months ago a friend pulled me back from the edge of the construction pit that had replaced Poe House. It was a depressing depression. I resolved to avoid that part of town. But really—the new manufacturing plant for lawyers is monstrous. It rises over the park, ruining the view south through Washington Arch, the classic Beaux Arts monument created by White in another era of this city. The law factory destroys the twilight framing of the campanile tower of Judson Church. It is a hulking presence rising there, over the vanished house where the bird flew in.

THE READER WILL PLEASE RISE AGAIN

We believe in the logos that kids who paint faces on them—believe in.

We believe that all advertising executives should be deposited in Tibetan caves with—hard-to-fathom gurus.

We believe that the TelePrompTer guiding the C student from Yale will suddenly show—the face of an Iraqi child.

We believe that if war is a petroleum product available at an affordable price then being in love must be— the dawn of the gift economy.

We can't believe that anybody ever managed—to put love up for sale.

We can't believe that Peace—can be secured by shopping weapons.

We believe Peace in all its forms has a chance—when the shopping stops.

We believe that we won't shop—until you don't bomb.

We believe that we won't shop—after that either.

Because by then we would've risen from the dead.

SIX

THE REVOLUTION IS MY HOT NEIGHBORHOOD

We've been malled and chain-stored so thoroughly that if a neighborhood is healthy—then it is politically radical. It stands out as a challenge. And evidence that a neighborhood is really happening is the unsupervised talk of a particular kind, by three people on a corner.

That sounds simple. It isn't. It's complex, and that is the point. For instance, you can't plan this; you can only get out of the way. You don't need Disney's model town of Celebration in Florida to prove that real neighborhoods cannot be made by the policies of corporations. The phrase "planned community" is oxymoronic. Do I have a witness?

We've seen three smiling talkers on the corner, and we've heard them too.

You can tell when the talking and listening are intense, even if it's a lazy and hot day. There is a jumpiness, an edge. If anyone is touching anyone else, that's a good sign, whether it is chest or shoulder slapping or touches on the hands. If one person listens with disbelief or exaggerated dismay on his or her face, if the group seems to exchange comic smiling masks, that's it. If the three seem to be in suspension while a story is acted out, and suddenly burst into laughter, that's the revolution right there.

I remember one time I was riding through Richmond, California. I left the east end of the weird San Rafael bridge. It was a Saturday, gray and windy. We were driving by a church where a funeral had taken place. There were three African American mothers in Sunday dresses and great hats—brims that went way out. Each of them had a white hanky, and with the wind shaking their dresses and their hats ready to fly off, each tended with her hanky to the face, eyes, cheeks, and nose of the lady to the left, talking and smiling as they did it, joined together in that circle.

Original individuals originate more original individuals, who generate a neighborhood that has that mix of comfort and surprise. Like our three talkers on the corner, originating people trade their stories artfully, but without the designation of an art form or the sponsorship of a corporation. The stories— and I mean to include shorter forms like jokes, memories, gossip, lies, insults, and even grunts—all have an agreed-upon drama. There is a presence of no-planning, of I-created-this-right-now, of an unknown at the climax of the tale. In my neighborhood the talk is hot because it is constantly unfinished, created now, aching toward something but subject to all the forces that the rest of us might push into it.

Paranoid police and transnational capital outlets share the message "Move along." A chain store creates a hush. In a verbal culture like New York, chain stores, full of awkwardness and Muzak, have no place in their place.

My suspicion that the neighborhood is the last worthy opponent of the transnationals comes first of all from how cor-

Supermodels are State Terrorism! Build this billboard and they will come!

porations act like sexually crazed adolescents around us. Picture the Starbucks scouts coming into a neighborhood and listening for the laughter, sneaking up on a diner and staring at us. The arriviste corporate folks tear apart neighborhoods every day with chain stores and malls, but the entire source of their aesthetic for the new antineighborhoods is what they just destroyed. Very love-hate, I'd say. Oh but they do crave happy people. They do expensive smile research. Then they broadcast smiles back at us until we're depressed. Exactly like the jilted lover who finally ends up banging you over the head with the roses. In a typical Kmart, nobody in the aisles is smiling, but the walls are covered with huge high-resolution grins.

Maybe a real neighborhood still exists—say, in the community garden near your home, or a near ghost town still there along Route 66, or a street corner in Washington Heights, or little communities up the Hudson or up the Pacific coast from San Francisco or along the water east of Mobile. Let's say you live in one of these places and someone tells you a story and you start grinning. Be careful, because a camera will find you— see it there in the window of that SUV? It's a location scout, an authenticity-hunter, an adperson. Your smile is raw material. Smiles, the facial expressions they cut and paste from the neighborhood, can be sold. Smiles sell.

Now—back to the emporium of bad soft porn that is my own neighborhood, because with who I am, children, I always have to return there. It's my neighborhood. Can someone help me? Keep it hot. Amen. In Noho, just uptown from Soho, like much of this part of New York, we are suffering from "development"—new buildings whose edifices come straight down to the sidewalks and don't afford a place to lean and talk. They want to keep us moving. Fewer stoops for human words.

We have rubble from demolition, and towering models sulking with sex quandaries rising from the vacant lots. The chain stores are coming in, high-end ones, with the falsely bright light and the hush of styled posing and no hot talk. The minimum-wage salespeople are unhappy and disconnected from the products on their shelves, which are covered with— you guessed—smiles.

Commodification leaves the neighborhood strewn with silent boxes of stylish air. The rents are so high that there's centrifugal spinning here, and a lot of people will fly off to outer Queens. The people who are selected to stay here are generally very tall white people. Their clothes are flown in from the same runways. Chinatown to the south is still a neighborhood, but all the Italian talkers who used to be around here have been sucked up into Scorsese films and haven't been seen since.

That's the thing that makes us suspect that the devil is in our midst, children. That flattening of natural hot chatter into white noise and big ads is evil. When you walk into the Starbucks at Astor Place there is no recognition; no one shouts "Yo!" or calls out your name. This is evil. There is a narrowing of the kinds of language that are shared in public, a regularization of gestures. It happens so gradually as a neighborhood dies that people only notice an untraceable emptiness, a certain dullness.

Can we say this? Whatever God du jour you are hanging with, don't go shopping. God wouldn't be in a chain store, I don't think. In fact, let's just say that GOD IS THE ABSENCE OF GENTRIFICATION. Let's add this to our beliefs next week. Someone give me an Amen. Because God really has to be interesting. Or let's make it rhyme for effect: God gotta be *Odd*.

You must have noticed, children, that I've been whipping ordinary living with words like "odd" and "hot." I've been circling around it, poking it, calling it lots of things. But three people talking on a corner should be just everyday life. So how did ordinary life become colonized? Lots of people have discussed with greater skill than I how the corporations conquered the last frontier, ordinary living. Please study the words of the saints: Tom Frank, Naomi Klein, Jean Baudrillard, Kalle Lasn, Benjamin Barber . . . we the anticonsumerists have produced powerful voices.

These writers have labored to explain a decisive phenomenon, brand manufacturing, where a company persuades us that a whole way of life is indicated by the sacred acceptance of a running shoe, a cup of burned-tasting coffee, a smiling rat. These writers, children, are Saints in the Church of Stop Shopping. With their help neighborhoods can stop their capitulation to the fierce, vague religious aura of these products. The common sense of individual and local self-reliance has not yet reached beyond traditional partisans—but it must, considering our emergency, reach the consumers themselves. At this point the agents of the products, the ubiquitous men in suits, flood our civic rooms with their disingenous theater. TV anchors routinely recite their press releases vertabim: "Analysts predict that with the new mall our county's economy will rise 15% in the first year. . . . "

Today let us ask these questions: How do we retake our life? How do we take back our neighborhoods? Let's talk practical politics. How do we revalue (or even notice) our commonest gestures and exclamations, remember our personal and public memories? So much of resisting transnational corporations is remembering things that we've been told to forget. What story do I have that isn't a part of a product's language? When my neighborhood's working, those are the stories that come up.

The revolution is just a neighborhood. Three talkers on a corner. Amen.

Can I tell my story? Can I take my time? All right, I'm going back to my neighborhood now. I'm walking into the Jones Diner. The diner has been there for sixty-five years, since 1938. The Olmstead development company is building multimillion-dollar luxury apartments on all sides and is in court trying to break the Jones lease. David Bowie moved in nearby. The supermodels are waiting in their limos in front of Balthazar and Prada. But so far George and Alex are still there in the Jones. They come in every morning from Astoria at 5 a.m.

One day I walk into the Jones Diner to have the stuffed-pepper special. I sit down. Now, there is an advertising campaign that put bright purple signs everywhere. Fairly small signs, featuring a single phrase in quotes, like someone is saying something. As I eat I find it hard not to read these things. I have about six of them in my field of vision. They have a friendly look, a very Smith Corona–ish old font—friendlier than e-mail fonts. The print is cheerily reversed out, white language on a purple background.

The messages of these six signs add up to what I call a "loneliness campaign." The signs' text reads like the offhand remarks of a close friend. In that tradition, some of the phrases seem almost aimless, like the way a buddy talks. So I'm sitting there in the Jones and I'm reading one of these signs. It says: "You mean she actually went up to your apartment?" That's it. Just that phrase, hanging there in the window while I'm having lunch. "You mean she actually went up to your apartment?" And so I'm thinking and saying—maybe my lips are moving— "Yeah, she did. Unbelievable."

Now, you may say that's harmless. Most ads, taken alone, are harmless. But here's my point: The people I am with in the diner are friends who would say this phrase to me in real life were the ad not there. After my kvetching about a relationship for weeks, Alex and George, who are right here now, would crow, "You mean she actually went up to your apartment?"

So while I'm eating today's special, stuffed peppers with boiled carrots—delicious, actually, and only six bucks—while I'm sitting there chewing, Alex notices that I'm staring at this sign. He traces the line of my gaze out the window. Maybe he notices the furtive arch of the eyebrow and small interior speech when I cooperate with the sign and have a full-blown memory of the disastrous visit by this young Parker Posey–cum–Audrey Hepburn figure to my fifth-floor pigsty, and then maybe Alex remembers me bringing her into the diner also, to a sort of general held breath. Maybe he's seeing all this in a flash and he's ready to intervene.

I'm daydreaming now, watching a full-scale movie of this visit that I'm projecting through the awful coffee steam, and Alex slaps me noninjuriously across the face. He's shouting, "Well, what was she thinking? I know I wouldn't ever go up to your place. First, what are the diseases? They've never been seen in this country, your diseases. I mean, we might read about your diseases in the news, but they haven't been seen around this neighborhood for years, what you got." George then comes over with "And then there's the insurance question. The rates for going up to your room would have to be worse than collision coverage in Jersey. What was she thinking? Send her over here so we can counsel the poor girl. I mean, she has no *idea*!"

Before long others in the diner, the usual motley human comedy, are assisting this routine with well-placed wisecracks. My ex-accountant is one of them, and a guy who runs a small furniture store nearby, Bob, chimes in too, although he always talks to me through the Reverend Billy persona: "Reverend, you're depressed again!" And of course I am in the sing-along myself: "Well, in fact she had very little idea. Up to that point she had done no meaningful research on what might happen, going up to my room." Around the diner people are shaking their heads slowly to empathize with what she must have experienced, like they are remembering what a great gal she was and how she was last seen with me, and to be in my arms is to be in some vast maw of purgatory.

We are acting out any insecurities I might have, a neighborhood full-court crowing contest, giving the clown back his catharsis. We are our own best audience, laughing to show how much we're liking our own wit but also laughing the way people do when collateral understandings, forgivenesses, and encouragements must be told by a parallel wink and a friendly pat.

Then the Odd, the unknown, arises. Alex, a Greek-American from Astoria who probably voted for Rudy Giuliani, drops to his knees and shouts, "But will you come up and see my etchings sometime? You've never been to my apartment." I'm taken aback. He's either laughing with or at gay culture, though I don't think he knows what gay culture is. But we're all laughing, and it's probably because he is a male male and we agree in the comedy that we're different. I'm a what—a gay heterosexual?—partly suspicious but somehow liked. But everyone in the long, narrow diner took trajectories to be here, everyone is suspect and grounds for a good-hearted suspicion.

I'm saying, "Well, I understand you have etchings featuring scenes of a famous diner." And he said, "Yes, different scenes, one with snow, one with just regular garbage everywhere . . ."

And Alex starts singing, crooning, like Vic Damone: "I etched my etchings in a night course at Cooper Union, just for you." George is playing air violin, heavy vibrato, and starts singing in his thick Greek accent, "I have diners on my walls just for you. . . ." And I'm thinking, Where is this going? And then suddenly a German tourist family appears in the door, all smiles, and we abruptly stop. Alex and George are instantly gracious and help them to a table.

A curious thing has happened, and I notice it later as I am walking home with my to-go bag. The labyrinth of joshing has saved me from the six purple signs in the windows. With the comic serenade of Alex and George, I can feel the signs shrink away. In fact, here's an important detail: *I can't even remember what those signs were selling. Amen!*

The hope for freedom starts in the body, in the psychic body. And in the configuration of three smiling talkers—as with Alex, George, and me encircled by purple signs trying to pass themselves off as confidants—we can leverage our way to freedom from the incoming seduction with the homegrown Oddness of our own conversation.

When you start with the hoped-for revolution, it's easy to keep wandering into military metaphors. But our revolution would not so much be an attack outward, because our opponent is not standing there in one place like the Berlin Wall. I understand our resistance as a claiming of the neighborhood, an honoring and strengthening of what we already do. Our opponent is everywhere and nowhere, does not have to retreat or advance. It melts into the air. And then it reappears, as it did that day. It was suddenly clear to me that their experts had been studying my loneliness. I would have been distracted for sure, lost in it, and sharing confidences with six purple signs, except I wasn't in a chain store. I was in the hot, Odd part of my neighborhood—and thank God.

I can't say that our guy rumble of cracking wise in the Jones, our shoving each other and acting desperate, constitutes any general strategy. But I suspect that anything I ever say about saving ourselves could be folded back into what happened that day in the diner. I know that the signs shrank away. And I know that somehow this comedy routine is the seed, the three-on-the-corner, the revolution, my neighborhood.

We have something in us that ad departments have an intense need for but which we ourselves have undervalued. They know that their seduction must find a way to interrupt Alex and George and me. Those purple signs nearly did. They came pretty close. The ad departments need to know exactly where the vast interior of the individual joins up with the mysterious souls of the other talkers. How do we instantly create these bonds? How do we do it without products? Where do our stories come from, anyway? They just seem to rise out of us magically. Oh, yes, the logo-driven must harness our brilliant banter, and this is as clear to them as placing a dam on a river for power.

The extraordinary is in the ordinary. The Odd pleasure rises through the trusting teasing that we offhandedly tend toward when we're together. In a ho-hum way we build a sneaky buoyancy in the room. We have to claim that in a more forthright way now, because they see it as a market. We have to claim it. We don't have to give them our power.

Thus ends today's message. Let us pray.

SEVEN:

THE SERIOUS CIRCUS

Immediately after the World Trade Center came down, people flocked spontaneously to Union Square, a mile north of the disaster. It is a historic meeting place for dissenters in the city. When I arrived there the park was already full of thousands of people, standing with candles, carrying flowers, talking to each other in hushed, somber voices. We stood without any agenda or any leader, and there were so many of us—out to Broadway, up to Nineteenth Street, and spilling down to Fourteenth, where the police barricades were stopping any traffic from going farther south. More people were arriving all the time, from the streets and avenues, in groups or alone, pouring in until there was a comfortable density of crowdedness. With each new person there came a candle and a willingness to lend flame to yours.

I snuck a look around. It occurred to me that no one present understood the exact nature of the event we were attending or what we were really doing there. There was no stage or sound system, no organized roster of speakers or bill of entertainers. But there was something going on at the center of the park. I was at about Sixteenth Street, on the west side, and I couldn't quite see—it was near the one-story-tall statue of George Washington with his arm outstretched, pointing down Broadway toward the mysterious double explosions that had transformed the landscape of the city.

Then I spotted a dull flash. A woman in a denim dress held a trumpet over her head, and it caught the candlelight. She was standing on a bench near the statue. She began to play an insistent, plaintive tune that rang out across the crowd: "God Bless America." A few people started to sing along. After she'd finished there was a pause and then she started up again, this time with "America the Beautiful." This struck a chord with the crowd, and everyone rushed to add their voices. Now we were fully rehearsed—we knew what this event was all about. You could see people singing from the balconies and roofs, and kids up in the crotches of trees. Congas were thumping on one side of the square. The park rang out with "For spacious skies, for amber waves," and we all joined in for "Amazing Grace," and then came the miracles. "I was blind but now I can see."

The flag was up the pole and unfurling before we even noticed we were deep into "The Star-Spangled Banner." The last two songs had let us fly across the country, from sea to shining sea. We had savored the simplest aesthetic of our country, the vertical flight that we insist on as optimistic Americans. Then, from this beautiful vast place on earth, with its purple mountains' majesty, we were all of a sudden blindsided by the rockets' red glare.

At the phrase "bombs bursting in air" thousands of the singers in our spontaneous choir went one way and thousands went another. The innocence that had emerged from the

The living and the dead join forces:
Union Square after 9/11.

wreckage of our tragedy was now officially over. Here and there in our strange, instant community, citizens stopped singing at the words that referred to bombing. And now began the remarkable time of Union Square in the fall of 2001.

There were little lost choirs of friends that began to try "Give Peace a Chance." Abruptly people stared. The old request for Peace died out, down to a last rude voice and was swept back into the anthem. General Washington's sharp arm rose above us like a missile launcher. General Washington was so brought to life by the martial melody that he seemed to be about to canter off down Broadway on his huge horse, trailed by lieutenants, not to return until he had defeated al-Qaeda and could wave triumphantly in the Canyon of Heroes.

The morning after the singing competition in Union Square, I lay on my back in bed, studying the paint flakes loosening from the sea-green ceiling. The ceiling was something to look at—its plaster was ladled in wave shapes that covered up beams supporting the floor above. It looked like an ocean that had been crudely painted by one of those folk artists from Maine. And this morning, mesmerized by my ocean view, I couldn't get out of bed. Maybe I was saving myself by noticing little things.

I wandered over to the window. The people down in the city were jaywalking at exhilarating angles, thanks to the God-sent absence of cars, which were being held back by those barricades up on Fourteenth Street. People were carrying themselves differently. I couldn't tell if they were slouching with sorrow or standing more erect because they had survived. They were certainly walking more slowly, that I can say for sure. I felt like I wanted to join them, so I went downstairs with Jessica. Everything was different. The sunlight on the ground floor, blasting us when the door opened, positively stank with toxic dust. The dog was blinking and sneezing.

How different was this, really? This is how different: The firefighters who had stood in line shouting in the Jones Diner on the corner were no longer there. Ladder 33 was located right next door on Great Jones. It seemed like just five minutes ago that the big guys had waited there at the counter shouting, "Milk, no sugar," always so at ease because they'd seen it all. Now I was daydreaming the length of the diner, feeling the presence of their absence.

It was strange. Our losses were searing. But in the face of the anguish you couldn't help but notice that the neighborhood was back. In the past few years it had suffered a long slide into yuppie silence. The once uproarious sidewalk life described by Walt Whitman had been quieted by deadly dark bars too hip to announce their identity with a sign out front. Packs of black-clad young whites marched out of the glossies, having marked Noho as their destination. They wandered in giggling gangs, asking the natives for directions to places we wished weren't here.

With the inconvenience of Tuesday's apocalypse they were all gone. Whole layers of new-money people were staying away. They had arrived here during the Giuliani years in their cars, which they stacked five high on pavement that had once been gardens. They parked and walked. They had a drinky date. They had their ritual, and it was a purchase. As they approached us from their condos, dominating our public space with their threats to buy, our neighborhood became a tunnel of eyes bearing down on us from billboards. One day in the summer of 2001 I realized that at the corner of Lafayette and Houston I was subject to the stares of thirty-four different models, all at the same time. That's sixty-eight eyeballs, some of them a yard across.

At the instant when the airliners sank into the towers, the supermodels retreated. It was as if they had backed up their runways into a vanishing point. They shut their orgasmic eyes. They no longer had permission to seduce us. We didn't even notice them for weeks and weeks. My attention came down off those walls, back to the streets, and back to you. There you are! Hello!

For that golden period we were no longer worshipers in the Church of Spacey Consumption. The leaders of the economic system that had transformed our neighborhood into a cloud of young consumers must have embroiled themselves in desperate conference calls during those days. Two airliners had cut us off from the ritual of making the purchase. For the first time in history, it became necessary for the president himself to ask us to start shopping again. I suddenly had the feeling that anything could happen. I went back to the Free Republic of Union Square, to say this loudly, to shout it, to shout with other shouters, to raise our voices into one organized song, to sing back at the smart bombs with computers in their nose cones whistling through the perilous night: Give Peace a Chance.

The world press was encamped around the edges of the square, the white bowls of their satellite dishes aimed up at the sky between the buildings. Brightly colored flags were by now draped over General Washington. A Dionysian compost of symbols and best wishes from around the world had poured into our acre, accumulating at the legs of his horse in pools of cooling wax and reverent tongues of flames. The eyes of the loved dead, staring at us from the homemade copy-shop posters, moon-gardened across the ground and up the lampposts and over the fences up the steps and across the paving stones of the plaza.

You couldn't skateboard straight through the park. You were slowed by the world's Godsightings.

The mourners from everywhere sent sacred objects and observations. Here are a few I remember: old leather-bound books and locks of hair, a music box featuring a pirouetting ballerina, place mats with faces and hearts drawn in the sky, poems and sheet music, heart-shaped brooches and small bulletin boards from the Midwest, hats and earth flags, hairpieces and jackets, small chests with latches, bodega candles, photos of the towers with angels added, illustrations of firefighters placing extension ladders up to heaven, a drawing of cows from Kenya, children's crayonings of the two towers (with one tower half the height of the other, like an older and younger sister).

Roses, mirrors, daisies, brocade, and lone lilies sprouted everywhere next to carefully copied out quotes from Gandhi, Gibran, Eleanor Roosevelt, and Dr. King. I remember something from a Texas cheerleaders' association that combined a saddle with a disco ball. Every kind of religious organization sent messages, but not just churches: 4-H groups, bowling teams, motorcycle clubs. A girls' water ballet troupe sent a giant card, I remember. Somebody sent a Polaroid picture of a river.

Many of these things had no obvious message that you could decipher. They were just personal things and seemed to have been pulled from the secret shadowy places of people, from attics and closets and who knows where. I felt that many things were owned by lost loved ones, sent here by surviving friends and relatives as an act of remembering. It was the Day of the Dead from all over the world, but no one I knew could figure out how the stuff got here. There was an agreed-upon postal destination: Union Square, put it under George Washington's horse. It happened on its own.

The now-daily immigrants to this place, Union Square, would gather around these precious things, and crowds would be studying them by midafternoon, an animated version of walking through an art exhibit. Always nearby someone was on their knees praying, small groups whispering intently, singing. Certain parts of the park became shrines, and other parts evolved into speaker's corners or break-dance emporiums. We would reflect and talk, forming confluences of volunteered paintings, dances, rap poems, political manifestos. Things sprang up very quickly and then died down and then rose again. Shy people would take the talking stick and pour out their feelings. And the people in the park were from every continent. The talking stick was waved in the air over many languages. The earth flag roped to General Washington's outstretched hand was accurate: These people were from the whole spinning rock.

And so it went on—discussion and ritual, unsupervised, unsponsored. It flooded into a new public space that opened up with the retreat of advertising and the rise of sheer chutzpah. The square had become a serious circus.

The intensity of the conversation came from the urgent questions we all were asking: How would revenge be taken? How could it be stopped? What could we propose in its stead?

We believed decisions had to be taken. We needed to form a response to the tragedy, find a definition of how being an American had changed. We insisted that this question mattered and that it was urgent. The American project wasn't working. Even as we talked, U.S. aircraft carriers were booting up their computers and snapping bombs to the underwings of their F-14s; immigration officials were seizing Americans and taking them to unmarked warehouses in New Jersey. The it-couldn't-happen-here-but-it-is-happening feeling was rife. We had to create a new direction, here, now, in this park.

No one was sleeping. The urgency was about peace, as if the 2,900 dead were watching us from the home-style photographs taped to every available surface by family and friends. You saw them carrying their photocopies and tape, renewing the faces after rainstorms. The loved ones left their dead with us, and they in turn energized us and broke down our easy answers, stopping us with their open smiles, joking at a backyard barbecue, holding up a terrier, laughing with a lover.

Their eyes held a secret that we hadn't figured out. I walked to the north end of the square, into the trees. The statue of Abraham Lincoln stood back there; he looked like he was deep in thought. At that end of the park there were smaller gatherings of folks, less inclined to join a debate. A Sufi group sat down on the grass and softly chanted for Peace.

But the lively dead eyes followed me all the way to the furthest end of being alone. I was standing in the middle of a thousand illegal candles. The flickering fire, reflecting on the stone ground of the plaza, made the color-copy eyes of the dead seem wet. They appeared to blink, watching me. They were talking to us, weren't they? What were they saying?

Their loved ones put words in their mouths. In Sharpie or computer fonts under their faces, there was a claim on life. Sandra is wearing her olive green dress today—tell her to call her family right away. The present-tense assumption of life at first felt sentimental, but then felt radically true. And there were thousands of them.

Theirs were not the only words. George Bush, posing with rescue workers at the sacred wreckage, made a speech that we listened to on radios in the park. The language of war descended on us like gas, the kind of talk that says nothing and only makes an impact. Words were released from the spinning war rooms, flown here in bomb bays from Missouri or Fort Benning. The language was instantaneously everywhere, the outrageous foregone conclusion of killing now made normal and sensible, read by the adolescent boy-king from portable TelePrompTers, which also urged him to put his arm around the closest representative of the FDNY.

The corner of Lafayette and Bleecker is the site of Walt Whitman's favorite watering hole, Schrafft's. I'd been experiencing his presence a lot lately. Maybe he was still holding forth around here. So I picked up *Leaves of Grass*, and in the manner in which certain books on certain days will turn your fingers and reveal themselves, the volume opened to "Song of the Departed."

These are deathbed farewell words, though Whitman lived for many years after he wrote them. Perhaps he understood that we are always in the last moments of our lives. He certainly loved opera and could write scenes of final farewells with aplomb.

Dear friend, whoever you are, take this kiss,
I give it especially to you—Do not forget me;
I feel like one who has done work for the day, to retire
    awhile;
I receive now again of my many translations—from
    my avataras ascending—while others doubtless
    await me;
An unknown sphere, more real than I dream'd, more
    direct, darts awakening rays about me—
So long!
Remember my words—I may again return,
love you—I depart from materials,
I am as one disembodied, triumphant, dead.

Walt chooses to ignore the devils and gods waiting in the unknown to wrestle over the design of his eternity. He simultaneously embraces the reader and the unknown that lies before him. It is an attitude that was adopted by many of those who perished in the towers on September 11. Calling their families on cell phones in the minutes after the planes had hit, they said, "I love you," and the power of their statement was released to us on the streets below. It's why our neighborhood suddenly came alive. Three talkers on the corner? We were everywhere. It was easy. It was necessary.

Whatever Peace is, it works in this mysterious language loop. Those messages in the last moments—*I hope you are well, I'm thinking of you, I love you, I will see you again*—on the cell, on e-mail, on answering machines, were not singing with hatred. In adopting those phrases—words that had become mere pop ditties, the schmaltz of Hallmark cards—the friends in the towers reclaimed them from the jealous grip of commercialization, where words of love have been held for so long.

Love. We are trained to think of it as a cheap all-purpose industrial material, like a polymer that can be heated up and cooled so that it fits snugly to the objects around it. For most of us it's been reduced to rich actors pretending to have sex on glowing silver walls, a flirtation that requires fifty takes in a Diamonds Are Forever advertisement. But love is a force, and it is a specific force.

In making their final declarations of love, the victims in the towers showed they were not afraid of death. They did not talk about it as if it were an opposing alien, a monstrous foreigner. As they looked at death they were reminded not of hate but of love. This assumed life survived in phrases beneath the Xeroxed gazes. The relatives continued talking in the miraculous present tense: Tell Eddie to call. We love him.

This is profoundly subversive for the commercial politician because once you are not afraid of death, maybe you won't want to shop, much less kill. Peace is an action at the edge of the unknown. That's what Peace is, a trusting response to the unknown.

In the last hours before the bombs began to fall in Afghanistan, we tried to keep these messages of Peace going. With the press around us, especially European, South American, and Asian, and noncommercial American TV, we gathered in a crowd before a big peace march. The reports of what the people in the towers said into their cell phones in the last moments were just coming to us through public reports and through friends and I spoke about them to the crowd. Those "I love you's" were meeting the present-tense demands in all the pictures taped everywhere. We were high on this conversation, and it carried through in our talking, too, this flood of intimacy.

So we need to project this—*I am alive, you are alive, I love you*—out ahead of the official talk, that other self-propelled language loop: *I am alive, you may be armed, I'll kill you first.*

We announced to the press that we wanted them to convey a message to Afghanistan, take something we would say out into the reflecting pool of media and get the waves washing all the way to Kabul. We started booming a chant, with the help of drums and musicians coming in: "I am alive, you are alive, we love you." Again and again and again.

Children of Peace:

Let us think about what happens to language in a war. Some of us feel that language is dulled, memory fades—there are varieties of censorship taking place right now that we feel but we don't know. Let's go back to a violent moment of this current war. Let's ask ourselves, what happens when a bomb falls?

When a bomb falls there, a bomb falls here.

Two mothers are having a conversation at sundown because this has been the time of day when the Americans have not been bombing. They are discussing the logistics of food, the closing of borders, the sleeplessness of children.

The mothers are talking in a Pashtun village square, and a bomb issues from the twilight sky. The airplane has flown nonstop from Missouri, and it cannot be seen. The decision to drop the bomb here is made at an office desk that is floating in a 6,000-ton war theater complex in the ocean to the south.

When a bomb explodes there, a bomb explodes here.

We wonder—what has happened to the American language? Where is its impact? Have jingoistic politicians and ad departments finally overwhelmed the common sense of talk? Has the surplus of overtrained actors in commercial messages finally made an honest emotion something we can't get across? What has happened?

We drop bombs to destroy original language. A bomb's language is as dumb and meaningless as the great belch of a murderer, and the conversation it is a part of only makes sense to other murderers with other belches, that is, other organizations with explosives.

The delicate singing language of the two Pashtun mothers is made this dumb. The bomb fell at the verb of one sentence, and the subject of that sentence is still in the air, hovering above the bomb crater. The subject of that sentence is still looking for its object, the completion of its meaning, in the compassion that mothers have regardless of the violence of the fathers. But the verb of the sentence is a hole in the ground thirty feet across. A piece of bright cloth floats down like a lost word.

This invisible muteness comes into our lives over here, where we pay taxes to make the jet, the computer, and the bomb. We don't know how the bomb comes back to us; we didn't think that it would. We don't see the bomb breaking our sentences until a surveillance camera tells us to shut up. We don't feel the explosive impact until the cop tells us to move along, or our Web site is black-holed, or a network anchor can't say the word "peace." Our original language is encouraged when we are apolitical—yes, then it's okay because it energizes the market—but any exercise in freedom is watched by recording devices, informers, security officials, and distant computers.

America is powerful because we can create stunned silence anywhere in the world. We make whole landscapes dumb and quiet. We are powerful because we are then free to fill the silence with our own words.

We move into that dumb silence with the second thing that comes down after the bomb. We move in with our replacement language. First, all the dumb silence in the gap between where the mothers stood and the computer on the carrier is now filled with the terrifying word "democracy."

Back here in the States that glorious word grows tired in our mouths. If we try to say the word in a prayer or a shout that carries too much of its original freedom, either it gets clogged in our throats because democracy now has a rancid, false taste to it, or we are stopped by others from speaking before it even has a chance to come out.

When democracy falls there, democracy falls here.

Bush expects the chants from the edge of his ground zero, but he has those miles of silence, huge dead-quiet shapes where there had been mothers, weddings, and great numbers of people, targets or not. He counts on that silence. That is where we must appear, looking into his eyes and saying, "Peace."

We can gather at Ground Zero, we can gather like we couldn't at Hiroshima. They are constructing fences and concrete and official park-service style plaques around the site. It's starting to look like an open pit mine inside a prison. But all around us are the God-things and faces of the dead, there in those pictures, insistently within an ordinary backyard moment. We have that funky laugh of Walt Whitman in Union Square summing up the continuing theme of the people in the towers, "I'll see you again."

Death in the unknown world of life doesn't act like a building that pulls in the fundamentalist pilots. Peace lets us cry and laugh with death, and spares us the distortion of going out and killing someone else. Peace allows us to remember our loved ones with a view unmediated by adolescent revenge. Death is more deeply complex than the cheerleading George Bush and should have a chance to be seen whole. See death whole and we don't have to shop for a distraction. Death seen whole has "I love you" in it.

THE PARABLE OF SELLING SOAP

Welcome to the church. I'm Reverend Billy. We are pre-Christian, we're post-American—let's go!

Today's lesson is a famous parable.

There was once an old father who had three sons, and the question (as always) was who would get the inheritance.

One day the father lined his sons up on the shore of the inland sea called Lake Michigan, for they lived there, near Chicago, and the father gave each son a small boat and instructed them in a voice between those of Jack Palance and Richard M. Nixon, "Go out into the world. The son who sells the most soap in one year's time will receive my blessings."

The youngest son's name was Roddy. He invented a soap called Irish Spring, and he hired a freckled Irish lassie to sell it. She grinned in sexual understanding at the TV viewer and said in an extreme Irish brogue, "Aye laddy, if y' take this bar 'f Irish Spring penis and ya rub it all over me like y'r tryin' to wash off me freckles!—Aye, then I'd be happy as a lark in sunshine for giv'n ya two more bars of soap for not half th' price!"

Roddy's soap business boomed. Irish Spring: a marital aid in disguise? a cream to prevent premature ejaculation? It was whatever the buyer wanted to project on that lassie's big grin, and a year later, as he landed his boatful of receipts at the old man's dock, Roddy reported, "Dad, I sold seven hundred truckloads of soap!"

"Well, my son, you'll never starve, but how could you take the grand old sod and tart it up for a bit of filthy lucre? You insult the memory of our dead grandma, God rest her soul."

"What? Dad . . . but no, no!" Roddy started gesturing wildly at the boat. "No, we've made a mistake, don't do it!"

But it was too late—Miss Irish Spring jumped out of the boatful of receipts like a stripper out of a cake and ran across the sand toward the old man, who had a look on his face like he'd just bitten into a piece of rotten meat.

She stopped. No one could move. It was all over—Roddy lost his inheritance.

The second son landed in his boat. His name was Bennett. He was smooth, self-possessed, and educated. In his boat he had one briefcase and three head-nodding vice presidents. He spoke in a modulated but efficient voice: "Dad, I commissioned studies with pie charts, percentages, tendencies—how high on the shelf do we place the soap? Where in the store in terms of the arc of the housewife's arm?"

As Bennett talked, the three vice presidents busily set up an overhead projector.

"Dad, this is my soap. I call it Icon. It's much more than a soap—it's a package. Look at the design. See that logo on the front? It's actually three logos in one. It combines the power icons of three civilizations—you see McDonald's golden arches, there, and the Nazi swastika, you can make it out right in there, and of course the Christian crucifix. Imagine the ecstasies, the havoc, the mass migrations, the millions of deaths caused by these three!"

He interrupted himself; the projector and screen were ready. He gestured with a remote clicker.

"Let me show you the results of our first field test. First picture. This is a supermarket in Dayton, Ohio, packed with perfect generic housewife consumers. See there, on the edge of the shelf, there's the Icon, bristling with unappeased power. And here we have the housewife, that's her generic boy, Jimmy. Here she turns her head and lets out a kind of hard moan, and grabs the Icon by its wrapping. 'Mommy's going to wash, Jimmy. Yes, Mommy needs a good scrub now . . . now.' And the boy cries, 'Mommy! Mommy!'

"Here's the consumer in a deep squat, her pupils dilating, screaming like a burger-flipping Nazi pope. She isn't using water. Father, she doesn't even need the soap. The soap isn't the point at all—she's washing with the package.

"She's prostrate now with package fever, the Icon on her like a pack of hyenas on a beleaguered water buffalo. The store manager screams and jumps into the Icon bath. Here a tour guide and a bus driver jump in. And now, running headlong from their bus, seventy-four tourists from Sun City, Arizona, disappear gasping and raving into a blur of Icon scrubbing."

The old man was such a proud father. He embraced and kissed Bennett, the corporate son.

"You, you have created power from the history of the world. Yes, I have decided—I will bestow my blessings on you, my child. I will buy shares in your company so that the housewives of America will make suds all day long while their husbands are at work. We will make a fortune, a soap opera on a scale never seen before. We'll be bigger than Palmolive, bigger than Tide and Cheer. We could shake hands on it now, but let's just wait and see what son number three has done, just to be fair. Don't worry, Bennett, you're the man."

So the old man waited with Roddy and his Irish Lassie and Bennett and his three vice presidents. A whole day passed, and when darkness came they left the beach. They went up the gray weathered steps to the house with its Cape Cod look and its deck at the top. They feasted on spare ribs with thick red sauce, barbecuing on the deck. They sipped their after-dinner drinks, the father and his two younger sons glancing out across the lake. Walter, the oldest son, was still nowhere to be seen.

The air grew cold and they trooped indoors, drunk and expansive. They sat and waited, uneasy in the strange silence. The lake weighed darkly in the windows. And then . . .

Off in the distance, on the swell of the dark inland sea, a light grew slowly, filling the house, shifting the shadows. The sons and the father got up and crossed to the windows, squinting, trying to make out a shape.

"It's not a light."

"It's a . . . no . . ."

"It's a boat. There's a light in the boat, but it's strange." The sons and the lassie and the vice presidents and the father rushed down to the water, where the spectral presence drew near. And then a haunting voice was heard.

"Father, Father . . . come on board, Father."

The vice presidents pushed Bennett, saying, "Your father—get him back indoors! He's bewitched! Don't let him go into the water."

But the old man had already waded in, wondering what that boat was made of. He was searching, trying to touch the great white boat of the third son.

Roddy and Bennett pleaded with him, "Father, come back to the house!" but already Walter had pulled him over the white bow. The sons and the lassie and the vice presidents grew smaller and smaller on the dark shore as the oldest son and his father sailed out to sea.

It was a clear night, the kind of night where it's easy to

tell the planets from the stars, and the points of light above reflected on the smooth waves. It was the kind of night where it dawns on you just how much is out there.

Walter set a bucket of water down in the center of the boat. Then he went to the mast and broke off a piece of it. He dropped it into the bucket . . . and it floated.

He looked at his father. "Ivory. Ninety-nine and forty-four one-hundredths percent pure. And it floats!"

The father stared at the bucket.

"Father, look at this starry night. Great things are up there, full of fire and ice, things that were there at the dawn of creation, forces that are too big to make any sense of. We design our gods after them, and our products, too.

"This boat is made of Ivory. It's ninety-nine—"

At this point the father interrupted, "What? Oh, that's what this is. Son, you made a boat out of soap! Well, soap sculptures are what children do. You have to make this soap useful—you have to sell it."

"No, Dad, you don't have to sell Ivory. It's pure. It floats."

"You should talk to Bennett. Maybe he'll give you a position in his company. He's already hired Roddy."

"Father, Ivory is the oldest soap. The sales pitch about purity and floating goes back into the last century: 'Step up close and give a listen, folks, and you'll remember this moment with gratitude for the rest of your born days . . . Purity, magical purity . . . with the glowing whiteness of an angel, this potion . . . caress yourself with it and fly, float, be pure. Go up into the air on gossamer wings . . . bless yourself with the elemental forces of nature.' The magic of this starry night here, that's the magic that Ivory has."

Walter's voice changed, became less lyrical, more sinister.

"Abraham was willing to kill Isaac, and God let Jesus die, and the Colonel let Elvis take those pills . . ."

"Son, what are you—"

Walter picked up the soap from out of the bucket. It glowed in the night. He grabbed his father and stared into his amazed eyes.

"O great white burning wind, nebulae, giant stars and comets, icebergs and white mountain fastnesses, I baptize my father, the last of the soap salesmen. I wash out his mouth, I clean out the selling, I shake out the market, so that we can move beyond him, into the world beyond America. . . ."

"Oh, no—haaaaahhhhh!"

"From this moment may Ivory soap not just pretend to be magic but actually receive its power from the great things up there, the pure floating light up there in the heavens. Amen."

And so, children, the next time that you are walking up and down those fluorescent aisles and you come to Ivory soap, join the thousands of consumers who have now turned supermarkets into millennial Stonehenges. Hold that bar up to the sky, praise God in heaven! Will someone give me an amen? Buy it as an act of sacred subversion.

Pick that bar of Ivory reverently off the shelf. Hold the Ivory in the air all the way to the register. "O great white burning wind, nebulae, giant stars and comets . . ." Let the customers know that this is the body of God, and march out there in a parade of worshipers who have liberated themselves from package fever. Bring the baggers and the security people and housewives and tourists into the street.

"I am water, and this is the body of God."

Oh, I feel the spirit in this room! (It's 99 $\frac{44}{100}$ pure!)

I'm Reverend Billy, bless you . . .

TWO-MINUTE RADIO SERMON: WHICH WAY TO HEAVEN?

We interrupt our regular programming for another moral advisory. I am Reverend Billy.

I live near the old St. Patrick's Cathedral on Prince Street, between Mulberry and Mott. This is the village common of my part of the city. The gravestones of the Irish, some of them dying so young in the 1800s, have the effect of taking the hurry out of a New Yorker. You look at the clouds, are surprised by an old memory or a new idea. As you walk along the famous sagging-inward red brick wall, the wonderful high trees seem to have been hurled into the sky by the lives that those dead lived.

One day, a four-story high rubberized billboard is unfurled down the side of an apartment building, right over the cemetery. On it is a gigantic sky-blue door with a Web site address. A phrase across it says, THIS WAY IN. It is an advertisement for an alternative heaven called Intel—this way IN. It towers over the dead and the living and addresses both with the same taunt.

Children, we must have a defense against this blue door. And our friends the dead—they give us that help. They seem to tell us "You are in. You are way in your life now. Don't open that blue door. It's not heaven. No one has to sell heaven."